Jasper Tudor: Brother & Uncle of Kings

A Tudor Times Insight

By Tudor Times

Published by Tudor Times Ltd

Tudor Times Insights

Tudor Times Insights are books collating articles from our website www.tudortimes.co.uk which is a repository for a wide variety of information about the Tudor and Stewart period 1485 – 1625. There you can find material on People, Places, Daily Life, Military & Warfare, Politics & Economics and Religion. The site has a Book Review section, with author interviews and a book club. It also features comprehensive family trees, and a 'What's On' event list with information about forthcoming activities relevant to the Tudors and Stewarts.

Titles in the Series

Contents

Preface

Jasper was the second son of the secret marriage between the widowed Katherine de Valois, Dowager Queen of England, and Owain Tudor. Favoured by his half-brother, Henry VI, Jasper became one of the Lancastrian dynasty's most stalwart supporters. He raised armies, besieged castles, spent years in exile, and never once changed his allegiance. Following the death of his nephew, Edward of Lancaster, at Tewkesbury, he showed the same loyalty to his other nephew, Henry Tudor.

Jasper was granted enormous estates in south-west Wales by his half-brother, Henry VI and spent considerable time and money on improving the castle at Pembroke, and the fortifications at Tenby. Yet, owing to the dire political situation, he was obliged to travel extensively across the country – fighting battles, fleeing pursuers, and besieging Yorkist castles. He seems to have been a master of the secret escape – even dressing as a peasant carrying a bale of straw once!

Jasper criss-crossed Wales, England, Brittany and France in his efforts to support his Lancastrian relatives – sometimes at the head of an army, but often as a fugitive.

It is difficult to believe that Henry Tudor would have achieved victory at Bosworth without the support he received from Jasper's Welsh connections, but Wales' involvement in the Wars of the Roses was not straightforward.

The material was first published on www.tudortimes.co.uk

Family Tree

Jasper TUDOR
Duke of Bedford

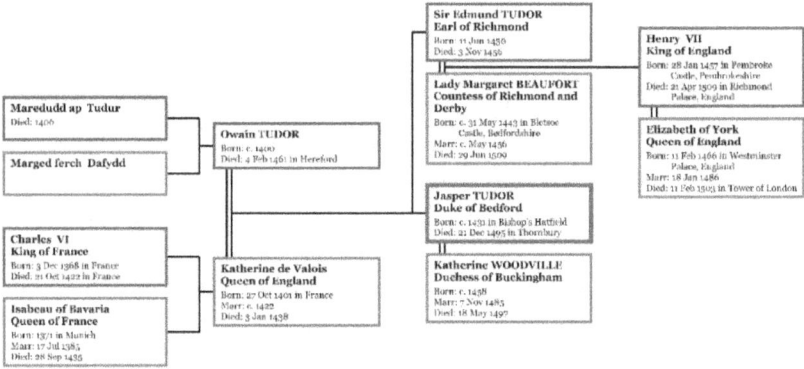

Maredudd ap Tudur
Died: 1406

Marged ferch Dafydd

Owain TUDOR
Born: c. 1400
Died: 4 Feb 1461 in Hereford

Charles VI
King of France
Born: 3 Dec 1368 in France
Died: 21 Oct 1422 in France

Isabeau of Bavaria
Queen of France
Born: 1371 in Munich
Marr: 17 Jul 1385
Died: 28 Sep 1435

Katherine de Valois
Queen of England
Born: 27 Oct 1401 in France
Marr: c. 1422
Died: 3 Jan 1438

Sir Edmund TUDOR
Earl of Richmond
Born: 11 Jun 1430
Died: 3 Nov 1456

Lady Margaret BEAUFORT
Countess of Richmond and Derby
Born: c. 31 May 1443 in Bletsoe Castle, Bedfordshire
Marr: c. May 1456
Died: 29 Jun 1509

Jasper TUDOR
Duke of Bedford
Born: c. 1431 in Bishop's Hatfield
Died: 21 Dec 1495 in Thornbury

Katherine WOODVILLE
Duchess of Buckingham
Born: c. 1458
Marr: 7 Nov 1485
Died: 18 May 1497

Henry VII
King of England
Born: 28 Jan 1457 in Pembroke Castle, Pembrokeshire
Died: 21 Apr 1509 in Richmond Palace, England

Elizabeth of York
Queen of England
Born: 11 Feb 1466 in Westminster Palace, England
Marr: 18 Jan 1486
Died: 11 Feb 1503 in Tower of London

TUDOR TIMES
© Tudor Times Ltd 2014

Part 1: Jasper Tudor's Life Story

Chapter 1: Childhood

Jasper was the second son of the secret marriage between Katherine de Valois, Princess of France and Dowager Queen of England, and one of the gentlemen of her household, Owain Tudor. He was born in around 1431, at the palace of the Bishop of Ely in Hatfield. Although the family are now referred to as Tudor, that was not how they were named at the time. Consistent with Welsh practice, which was merely to designate a child by his or her father's name, Owain was known as Owain ap Maredudd ap Tudur (Owen, son of Meredith, son of Tudor in English) and Jasper and his older brother Edmund were referred to as Jasper and Edmund ab Owain or, sometimes, as Jasper or Edmund ap Maredudd

When Jasper was around five years old, his mother died of a lingering illness in Reading Abbey, and his father was almost immediately imprisoned for the offence of marrying the Dowager Queen without consent. Jasper, Edmund, and possibly a couple of younger siblings, were given into the wardship of William de la Pole, Earl of Suffolk. Suffolk was a rising star at the court of Jasper's half-brother, Henry VI, King of both England, and, theoretically, France.

The Tudor children (as we will call them from now on) were placed in the care of Suffolk's sister, Katherine, Abbess of Barking, and remained there for the next ten years. They were paid for by Henry VI, although the fees were often somewhat in arrears and the Abbess was obliged to write urging payment in 1440 of £52 12s to cover previously incurred costs. A final payment for the Tudors' keep was made in February 1443. It amounted to £55 13 s 4d to cover expenses up until March 1442.

It's likely that the last payment was made to 1442 because this was the time that Jasper and Edmund were received at court by their half-brother King Henry VI of the House of Lancaster. The brothers were both knighted in 1449, Edmund on the 15th and Jasper on 25th December.

Different biographers have varying views of how much of the traditional military training the Tudor brothers received. It seems unlikely that if they were at Henry VI's court they would not have received similar training to that of other young nobleman – physical training in riding, wearing armour, fighting with sword and lance and military strategy. However there are no records of exactly what education Jasper might have had.

Four years before Jasper came to court, Henry VI had married Marguerite of Anjou. Marguerite was 15 years old and niece by marriage to Charles VII of France. Charles VII, being the brother of Katherine de Valois, was, of course, Jasper's uncle but Marguerite was his wife's niece and therefore far more distantly related to Jasper. Nevertheless this familial connection may have played a part in Jasper's later loyalty to Marguerite.

Henry's marriage was deeply unpopular. England's hold on France had disintegrated and the blame for this was laid squarely at the door of Henry and his closest advisers, perhaps not altogether fairly. Whilst Henry was the least military of kings, it is hard to imagine that any English King, even Henry V, could have held France once the Burgundians and Armagnacs had given up their civil war and united under the determined rule of Charles VII. France was larger, more populous, and eventually, wealthier. Additionally, once the generation of men who had fought beside Henry V– his brothers, the Dukes of Bedford and Clarence and the Earls of Shrewsbury and Salisbury - were dead, there was no-one who commanded sufficient skill or resources to replace them.

During Henry VI's youth and early reign, the court was largely divided into two factions - the Peace Party, initially led by Henry Beaufort, Cardinal of Winchester (Henry VI's great uncle) and the War Party by, headed by Humphrey, Duke of Gloucester, the last surviving brother of Henry V. Gloucester was closely allied to Richard, Duke of York who, on Gloucester's death, in somewhat suspicious circumstances in 1447, became Henry VI's nearest male heir. York was one of the few men surrounding Henry VI with any military talent at all.

Henry VI was of a pacific turn of mind and the Peace Party triumphed, arranging the marriage with Marguerite to cement a truce, ceding the county of Maine, and accepting the bride without a dowry. This was seen by the War Party as a disgraceful alliance and Marguerite was, accordingly, resented from her first appearance in England, and her failure to conceive (it was always the woman's fault) for seven years after her marriage was also a problem.

York was disgruntled. He felt overlooked; when his struggles to maintain English control of Normandy were not appreciated, his considerable costs were not reimbursed, and he was now likely to be relegated from his position as the King's heir. Marguerite, used to the factional politics of the French court, was suspicious of York from the start, seeing his position as Henry's heir as a threat.

It was agreed that the Duke of York would be appointed as Lieutenant of Ireland for a period of 10 years. On paper this was a prestigious office but it was obvious that the purpose was to remove York from the soil of England and Wales. Lords Lieutenant were not permitted to return without leave from the King. York eventually departed in June 1449, but returned in September 1450.

Chapter 2: Wealth & Position

There was unrest at the lower levels of society as well as amongst the nobles. In a rather schizophrenic world view, the costs of the war with France and the necessary taxes that had been raised to pursue it were resented, whilst failure to prosecute the war vigorously and the peace settlement related to the King's marriage were also resented.

Personal as well as political rivalry lay between Richard of York and Edmund Beaufort, Duke of Somerset. Somerset was far closer to the King and Queen than York and his appointment as Lieutenant in France had outraged York who felt it undermined his own position as Lieutenant in Normandy. Particularly galling was the fact that Somerset was well provided with men and funds whilst York had insufficient supplies.

Had Somerset been successful in his campaign, matters might have turned out differently. However he was not a competent soldier, and failed to achieve anything. In the north, as well, the Percys and the Nevilles were constantly feuding. York's closest ally was his brother-in-law, Richard Neville, Earl of Salisbury, and this pairing made it almost certain that in any dispute, Henry Percy, Earl of Northumberland would support the opposite side from York.

In 1450 – 1451, Parliament was restive. To improve the Crown's financial position many of the grants of land that had been made in the previous 20 years were cancelled in an Act of Resumption (which 'resumed' previous crown ownership) but this did little to help the growing unrest in the country which was becoming increasingly lawless.

In 1452, the Tudor brothers were both granted earldoms, the first men of Welsh blood to be ennobled by an English King. Edmund received the earldom of Richmond and Jasper that of Pembroke. Their status was high – as the King's uterine half-brothers they were granted precedence above all other earls, preceded only by the royal dukes – York, Buckingham, and Exeter. Although Jasper was not a member of the English Royal family by blood, he was granted the right to bear arms the same as the King's, differenced by a border of martlets. It was quite clearly stated in the Parliamentary Act that created them that Edmund and Jasper were *'the natural and legitimate sons of the same most serene lady the queen'*

Pembroke was a large and valuable earldom – it was a County Palatine which gave its earls a far higher degree of autonomy and responsibility for administration in their designated lands than in ordinary earldoms. Unfortunately however, because the earldom had been in royal hands since 1450, some of the lands related to it had already been granted to Queen Marguerite as part of her jointure. Jasper was granted cash by way of compensation. The grand ceremony at which Edmund and Jasper were publicly invested as earls took place on 6th January 1453 – the Feast of the Epiphany.

The brothers could now be summoned to Parliament as barons, and Jasper attended the opening session at Reading of the 1453 Parliament, on 6th March. By this date, an arrangement had been made to replace Queen Marguerite's holdings within the earldom of Pembroke with other sources of income and the lands were granted to Jasper. The majority of these lands were based around Pembroke Castle in south-west Wales together with holdings in London. These grants of valuable earldoms did not help Henry VI's finances, but it was important for the King to have loyal family. Following Gloucester's death, Henry's closest relatives were his half-brothers. His next nearest relatives in England were the Duke of

Exeter and the aforementioned Edmund Beaufort, Duke of Somerset, both descendants of John of Gaunt.

Somerset had had an older brother, John, who had died in 1444 leaving a daughter, Margaret, now heiress to great estates. As another mark of favour, and an opportunity to increase the income of his half-brothers, without cost, Henry granted the wardship of Lady Margaret Beaufort to Edmund and Jasper, jointly, in March 1453. This was a perfectly normal transaction and permitted the guardians to draw the income of the ward's estates until the ward reached maturity. The guardian was also free, within limits, to arrange the marriage of the ward. The usual practice was for the guardian to either marry a female ward himself or arrange for a marriage to one of his own offspring. In this particular case, despite the youth of Margaret, she was married to Edmund six months after reaching the legal minimum age of 12. There do not seem to have been any plans at this time for Jasper to marry.

Chapter 3: Storm Clouds

In August 1453, Henry VI fell into a catatonic stupor, failing to recognise anybody or respond to any stimulus. This left a huge void in a state reliant on personal rule. The obvious choice, in his own mind at least, for the role of Protector or Regent was Richard, Duke of York. Unfortunately the factionalism of the previous 15 years meant that he was by no means a unanimous choice. In particular Queen Marguerite, who was delivered of a son in October 1453, and her close associate, Somerset, rejected the idea. Jasper, however, seems at this time to have had a good relationship with York and to have been willing to work with the Duke.

Jasper attended a meeting of the Council on 21st November 1453 at which York had petitions to free imprisoned men of his affinity accepted and at which his associate, the Duke of Norfolk, presented a bill complaining about the incompetence of Somerset. Jasper was also present at another Council meeting in December which put forward York as Protector. But, since the Council was not complete, it did not have sufficient authority to install him.

Despite the best efforts of Queen Marguerite and his doctors, Henry could not be restored to health – even failing to respond when he was presented with his newborn son. By February 1454 the King's health could no longer be hidden. Parliament resumed and considered petitions from both York and Queen Marguerite, who claimed the regency on behalf of her son.

Although there were precedents in European countries for queens to act as regent, no English queen had been regent for a minor child, and with Marguerite herself being so unpopular it was unlikely that the experiment would be tried on this occasion. Parliament appointed the Duke of York as Protector of the Realm in April 1454. As far as can be ascertained, Jasper was in favour of this decision. York did not have free rein, but was constrained to act within certain limits.

Over the next few months, York seems to have made a genuine effort to exercise his Protectorate impartially, with the exception of the imprisonment of the Dukes of Somerset and Exeter. Exeter had once been York's ward, and was married to his eldest daughter, Anne, but there was no love lost between the two men. Jasper was present at a number of the Councils called during the year 1454 by York to improve administration and presumably took part in debate and discussion.

At Christmas 1454, Henry VI made a sudden recovery. Subsequent events suggest that, although he recovered his senses insofar as regaining his memory and his ability to function in day-to-day terms, his mental acuity was severely damaged. From this time forward he was even more dependent on his wife.

Orders were immediately given for the Duke of Somerset to be released from the Tower of London. The officials that York appointed – his brother-in-law, Richard Neville, Earl of Salisbury as Chancellor and the Lord Treasurer, John Tiptoft, Earl of Worcester, were replaced with allies of the King and Queen and the captaincy of Calais, which York had taken for himself, was granted to Somerset in an act which appears deliberately provocative. In defence of Queen Marguerite we should bear in mind that she genuinely feared that York sought to displace her son.

Lines were now being drawn – York's closest allies were Salisbury and the latter's son, the Earl of Warwick, but the vast majority of the nobility still retained its loyalty to Henry VI. Jasper swore a new of allegiance to the King and, despite having supported York's government and attempted to reconcile the parties, he now firmly nailed his colours to Lancaster.

It impossible to know the specific considerations that led any of the protagonists to support one side or the other when they were all closely related, and well-known to each other, but we can perhaps believe that Jasper felt gratitude, loyalty and affection for his half-brother, even though he knew him to be an inadequate King. No doubt Jasper hoped that the young Edward, Prince of Wales, might be a more effective ruler when his time came.

Chapter 4: 1st Battle of St Albans

York was still not aiming for the Crown itself, he merely wanted to control the King's government. He was summoned, together with Salisbury and Warwick, to appear before a Great Council of the other nobles to explain his actions. He wrote to the King, protesting his loyalty, but headed towards London with a small army. It is unclear whether his letters of explanation ever reached the King, who had left London. It is unlikely that the King's party were expecting an armed confrontation and most of his supporters were accompanied only by their usual household retinues, but on 22nd May 1455 when the King's party reached the town of St Albans, they were greeted with the news that York and his supporters were in the vicinity with an armed force.

Discussions between the two groups broke down – even the gentle Henry VI was moved to anger by York's attempts to run his government. The town was barricaded by the Lancastrians but in a surprise move led by the Earl of Warwick – a talented and ruthless soldier – the Yorkists broke into the town through an unguarded route. The Duke of Somerset, the Earl of Northumberland and Northumberland's nephew, Lord Clifford, were killed and most of the other Lancastrian lords injured to a greater or lesser degree. It is not known whether Jasper fought in the battle but, according to his biographer, Dr. Sara Elin Roberts, he was captured after the battle, along with Buckingham and the Earls of Devon and Dorset – the latter was Somerset's son, Henry, and now became 3rd Duke of Somerset. The King himself was slightly injured and carried back to London under the control of York.

With Somerset now dead, York became Constable of England and Salisbury and Warwick were confirmed as Guardians of the West Marches of Scotland. This was a move that was likely to anger the new

Earl of Northumberland (who was Salisbury's nephew – his mother, Eleanor, being Salisbury's eldest sister). The rivalry between the Nevilles and the Percys for power in the north had been a significant factor in the unrest of the 1440s and 50s.

Both Jasper and Edmund were summoned to Parliament for July 1455. In the months between St Albans and the July Parliament, Jasper had remained in London, despite the withdrawal of Henry and Marguerite to Hertford, just north of the capital, and had continued to negotiate with York.

The Parliament of 1455 again attempted to claw back some of the money lost to the Crown over the previous years with another Act of Resumption. Fortunately for them, the lands granted to both Tudor brothers were exempt. On 24 July 1455 Jasper again swore allegiance to his half-brother.

The extent of the lands that Jasper had been granted, together with his joint responsibility for the wardship of Lady Margaret Beaufort, made him the equivalent in modern terms of the Chief Executive Officer of a large, multi-million pound business at around the age of 24. He had a Council to manage his lands and receive his rents, and was also allowed to have a personal household within the King's court consisting of a chaplain, two squires, two yeomen and two chamberlains.

Jasper's Council included a number of men who were later involved in the Wars of the Roses – some as Lancastrians but others as Yorkists. His Councillors, the majority of whom were Welshmen, or from the Marches of Wales, included Thomas Vaughan, Geoffrey Pole and William Herbert. Vaughan was also a Squire of the King's household and was the administrator of Edmund Tudor's estate following the latter's death in 1456. Vaughan and Herbert were members of York's affinity – holding lands in York's vast Mortimer estates in the Welsh Marches, but at this point, no conflict of loyalties seemed likely.

When Parliament met again in November 1455, Jasper, although summoned, did not appear and nor did Edmund. Stern letters were sent out to both of them, and the other peers who had failed to put in an appearance, and they were commanded to attend the next session, which opened on 14 January 1456, by which time Parliament had again appointed York as Protector, although he was dismissed in February 1456, even though, in an attempt at conciliation, a number of his allies remained in Henry's government.

Chapter 5: The Phoney War

During this period, both Jasper and Edmund were busy in South Wales. Despite his earldom being based in Richmond in Yorkshire, Edmund now appears at the Bishop of St David's Palace of Lamphey in Pembrokeshire with his young wife, Lady Margaret Beaufort, attempting to restore order to the principality. It is not clear whether, initially, he was there under the orders of the King and Queen or of York.

One of the key troublemakers (in government eyes) in Wales was Gruffydd (English – Griffith) ap Nicolas of Dinefwr. Gruffydd held a number of high offices in South Wales – Deputy Justiciar and Deputy Chamberlain at different periods and, supported by his sons, Thomas ap Gruffydd and Owain ap Gruffydd, was treating his lands as a personal fiefdom. During 1454, York as Protector had ordered Gruffydd to release someone he had been holding, illegally, in Carmarthen gaol. The promotion of the Tudor brothers was intended to counterbalance Gruffydd's power.

Edmund's attempts to control Gruffydd were as futile as those of York had been and by June 1456 there was almost open warfare between them. By this time, Edmund was definitely acting on the authority of Henry, which may have led to York seeing him as a potential threat, rather than an ally,

Gruffydd had control of the castles of Aberystwyth, Carmarthen and Carreg Cennen, despite the fact that York was, in theory, constable of all three of them. By early 1456 Edmund had wrested Carmarthen Castle from Gruffydd. This put York in a difficult position as it appeared that Edmund was undermining his own power.

York therefore decided to move against Edmund and in this he was supported by two of Jasper's previously mentioned Councillors, Thomas Vaughan and his half-brother, William Herbert, together with Herbert's father-in-law, Sir Walter Devereux. At what point these three decided to transfer their allegiance entirely from Jasper to York is unclear. Originally there had been no need to choose between Jasper and York as the two men were on good terms but now the situation was deteriorating.

Herbert and his men led a considerable force against Carmarthen Castle and captured it, imprisoning Edmund. They then moved on to Aberystwyth which they also successfully subdued and returned to York's control. As all of these castles were in fact royal castles, this gave York command of government in South Wales.

Meanwhile, Jasper was back in London undertaking commissions, together with the Dukes of Exeter and Buckingham, to suppress rioting in London, Kent, Sussex and Middlesex. He spent a good deal of his time with Henry at Sheen and at Windsor, and then with the royal couple at Coventry.

Coventry was in the centre of Queen Marguerite's own lands and she was spending significant amounts of time in the area, as well as money on restoring her various castles there. It is this change in focus from London to Coventry that Chris Skidmore in his book '*Bosworth*' cites as one of the reasons for the Londoners becoming increasingly disenchanted with the Lancastrian government and preferring York, who always favoured the capital.

Herbert and Devereux were summoned before the Great Council at Coventry in September 1456 to answer for their actions in relation to the capture of Carmarthen and the other royal castles. The Council recommended that they be imprisoned. Devereux was sent to Windsor and Herbert was supposed to be dispatched to the Tower of London but managed to slip away to Aberystwyth Castle where in October 1456 he began to raise an army. He was declared a traitor and a reward of 500 marks was posted for his capture.

Gruffydd ap Nicolas was granted a pardon on 26th October by the Queen as she made a progress through the Marches. This secured Gruffydd's allegiance to Lancaster. York's allies were also being replaced in government with the posts of Lord Treasurer and Chancellor being taken by the Earl of Shrewsbury and Bishop Wayneflete of Winchester respectively. Queen Marguerite's own Chancellor also became Keeper of the Privy Seal. This effectively returned government to supporters of Henry and Marguerite and left the Yorkists out in the cold.

Chapter 6: Search for Reconciliation

On 1st November 1456 Jasper suffered the loss of his brother Edmund. It is not clear what Edmund died of - almost certainly natural causes. However it may be that Edmund's brief imprisonment by York's followers, which can hardly have improved his health, led to Jasper becoming more firmly attached to the Lancastrian cause, and sowed the seeds of rivalry with Herbert and Vaughan.

Jasper now took over Edmund's responsibilities in South Wales, and also complete responsibility for his widowed countess, Margaret, who was expecting a child. Margaret moved to Jasper's own castle of Pembroke to await the birth, which took place on 28th January 1457. The boy was named Henry. Because Edmund had no adult heir, his lands reverted to the Crown for the period of the young Henry Tudor's minority, with an annual dower granted to Lady Margaret.

Another Great Council was held in Coventry about a month after Henry was born, which Jasper attended.

Following the Great Council, the court moved to Hereford. This was more or less in the heart of York's Mortimer lands, which comprised great swathes of the Welsh Marches and was perhaps a symbolic act to show the Queen's dominance.

Meanwhile Jasper and his widowed sister-in-law were visiting Humphrey, Duke of Buckingham, in order to arrange a new marriage for Margaret with the Duke's second son, Sir Henry Stafford. Whilst Margaret's marriage would reduce the income that Jasper could take from her estates (she was still a minor) it would give her and her son an additional measure of protection. It was not unknown for heiresses to be abducted and forcibly married, so it was far preferable for Margaret to ally with fellow Lancastrians of high birth.

Jasper's exact whereabouts over the next few months are unknown. He next appears at the famous Loveday event of 25th March 1458. The Loveday was a mediaeval practice whereby warring parties were publicly reconciled. Henry VI no doubt hoped for great things from the public reconciliation of Queen Marguerite with York, but in this as in much else, the King was naive. Jasper probably took part in the ceremony, but there are no specific accounts of his presence.

Lovedays were all very well but practical measures for maintaining defences were required. During 1457 - 1458 Jasper was closely involved with the re-fortification of the town of Tenby, on the coast of south-west Wales. Jasper shared the cost of rebuilding the walls and repairing the moat with the townspeople. Tenby, although almost as far from the seat of English government as anywhere in the kingdom of England and Wales, was well-positioned as a port from which ships could ply between Scotland, Ireland, France, Brittany, Cornwall and Wales. He also improved the fortifications at Pembroke.

On 8th January 1458, five days after the marriage of his mother to Sir Henry Stafford, the wardship of Henry Tudor, Earl of Richmond, was granted jointly to Jasper and John Talbot, Earl of Shrewsbury. This, together with the reversion of those of Edmund's lands which had been held in survivorship by the pair, gave Jasper an income of around £1,500 - in a period where only the richest nobles had incomes greater than £1,000 and a gentleman could survive comfortably on £20 per annum. The very richest nobles of all, such as the Dukes of Buckingham and York, had estates and income to the value of around £3,500 per annum. Of course, much of this income was on paper and not always easy to collect. To counterbalance the income, Jasper had significant expenses in the maintenance and upkeep of his castles.

Chapter 7: The Slide into War

In the Parliament of 1458 Jasper, together with 59 other peers of the realm, again swore allegiance to King Henry VI. In an effort to reconcile the parties, an act of indemnity was passed absolving the Duke of York, the Earls of Salisbury and Warwick and their supporters, of any responsibility for the Battle of St Albans, which was conveniently blamed on deceased peers.

Despite this, low-level warfare continued. In April 1459 Jasper took control of the disputed Carreg Cennen, Carmarthen and Aberystwyth castles but was subject to attacks from the Sir John Dwnn, a cousin of Gruffydd ap Nicolas and another of York's retainers.

Further trouble also broke out when the Earl of Warwick, who had been granted the post of Captain of Calais, but was left short of funds, was recalled to England to explain to the King why he had indulged in piracy against the merchant ships of the Hanseatic League. Warwick's actions were popular with the public as they reduced the competition for English wool, however they led to an increased risk of Continental war which was against official government policy. Warwick's men brawled with the King's household and he himself returned to Calais without answering the charges, claiming that his life had been threatened.

The court again moved towards Coventry and Queen Margaret began to recruit forces. At this time the use of the red rose to symbolise the House of Lancaster was not common, and instead badges of the Silver Swan designated loyalty to Henry, Marguerite and their son Edward, Prince of Wales. The Council was summoned to Coventry for 24th June 1459. York, Salisbury and Warwick were summoned but, fearing that they would be arrested, they refused to attend. This was in open defiance of the King and the Council indicted them for treason. The Yorkist Lords and their retainers were geographically divided – Salisbury was based at Middleham Castle in North Yorkshire and York, together with his wife, Cicely, and children, was at Ludlow in the Welsh Marches. Both of them began to raise forces.

Thus Queen Marguerite's choice of Coventry as her powerbase shows her strategic grasp of matters – her forces were between the two main Yorkist groupings. Warwick landed from Calais in the south of England and began to march towards his estates in the southern Midlands. Before he reached Warwick, he turned west towards Ludlow to meet up with York whilst his father, Salisbury, tried to reach Ludlow bypassing to the north of Coventry and then heading down the border between England and Wales. Salisbury's forces were intercepted by the Lancastrians under Lord Audley at Blore Heath in Staffordshire.

Throughout the Wars of the Roses the Yorkists showed themselves to have superior commanders, winning more of the set-piece confrontations, although they seldom had as many men as the Lancastrians. At this battle, despite Lancastrian superiority of numbers, Salisbury's tactics won the day and he arrived at Ludlow to meet up with York, Warwick, Andrew Trollope, who was one of Warwick's captains, Grey of Ruthin and Sir Walter Devereux. Sir William Herbert did not join York on this occasion.

However the Lancastrians were in full pursuit, and had the added advantage of the presence of the King. Not that Henry VI was of any use as a battle commander, but his presence inhibited many men from taking arms against him. Henry was also supported by the sons of the men killed by the Yorkists at St Albans – Henry, 3rd Duke of Somerset, and Henry, 3rd Earl of Northumberland. It does not seem that Jasper was with the Royal army which encamped at Ludford Meadows, on the opposite side of the River Teme from Ludlow. It has been suggested by his biographer Terry Breverton that instead, he was guarding the road to Ludlow from the west to prevent Welsh Yorkists from reaching the town.

Once again pardon was offered to those in the Yorkist ranks who would return to their allegiance to Henry VI and this offer was taken up by Andrew Trollope – Trollope was an experienced military commander and his loss was a serious blow to York as he commanded the men brought from Calais by Warwick. Trollope remained one of Lancaster's most devoted adherents until his death at Towton.

In an act of self-preservation that is hard to respect, York, Salisbury, Warwick and York's two sons, Edward, Earl of March and Edmund, Earl of Rutland, deserted their army to save themselves, slinking away at night. Salisbury, Warwick and March sailed for Calais, whilst York and Rutland took ship for Ireland, with Jasper's men hard on their heels.

York's Duchess, Cicely, and her younger children, were put into the custody of Duchess Cicely's sister, Anne, Lancastrian Duchess of Buckingham. The remaining Yorkists submitted to the King. In an act which hugely undermined the Lancastrian cause, Marguerite allowed her troops to plunder Ludlow.

Chapter 8: Triumph of York

Yet another Parliament was held in Coventry in November and December 1458, which became known as the 'Parliament of Devils'. Jasper attended, although he arrived somewhat late. Once again, all of the nobles present swore allegiance to Henry VI and Edward, Prince of Wales. York, Salisbury, Warwick, March, Rutland and their key followers were attainted of treason and had all of their estates forfeited.

Jasper himself and his father Owain, of whom nothing had been heard for some time, were rewarded with new estates. Owain was knighted and granted a number of manners in Kent, Sussex and Warwickshire. The following April (1459) Jasper received the accolade of being elected as a Knight of the Garter and was also granted, for life, a tower in the Palace of Westminster for his Council meetings and archive storage.

Despite the apparent resurgence of the Lancastrians, the underlying problems of a weak King, an unpopular Queen and quarrelsome nobles had not been overcome and the fighting continued.

In early 1460 Jasper was appointed for life to the position of Constable, Steward and Master Forrester of the Lordship of Denbigh in North Wales, close to the coast. Denbigh had previously been one of York's castles, so needed to be held by the Lancastrians to prevent York entering the country by sea from Ireland. The castle garrison resisted, remaining loyal to its former constable and Jasper was obliged to besiege it. In order to subdue the castle Jasper requested consent from Henry VI to issue a commission to raise troops, to pardon any members of the Denbigh garrison who were prepared to submit and to execute those who would not submit. He also requested permission to distribute any of the contents of the castle, once captured, to pay his followers.

These permissions were granted by Letters Patent on 22nd February and Jasper proceeded to raise forces, led by a number of Welshmen from South Wales. Jasper also received a grant of 1,000 marks to cover the costs of the campaign, to be derived from York's former holdings in the marches. By the end of May, the castle had fallen – the first time in its history that it fell to external attack.

Meanwhile forces were being raised by both Lancastrians and Yorkists, which met at Northampton on 10th July 1460. The Yorkists, led by Warwick, gained the victory, helped by the treachery of Lord Grey of Ruthin who, despite being in the Lancastrian army (having been pardoned after Ludford Bridge) gave orders to his men not to fight.

Three of the most senior Lancastrian captains were killed – the Duke of Buckingham, Lord Egremont (brother of the Earl of Northumberland) and Viscount Beaumont. The Yorkists captured King Henry. Queen Marguerite, hearing the news of the King's capture, was unable to raise further troops and crossed speedily into Wales with her son.

Now in control, the Yorkist Lords marched into London. York declared to Parliament that he was the rightful King of England as he was descended from the second son of Edward III, rather than from the third son, Henry VI's ancestor. The Duke was met by stunned silence. Controlling a weak King was one thing – overthrowing him entirely, was completely different.

Parliament however recognised York's superior genealogical claim and declared that whilst King Henry would continue to rule for the remainder of his life he would be succeeded by York, rather than by his son Edward, Prince of Wales. Henry had little choice but to accept this act, which was passed on 24th October 1460. It was also agreed that York would immediately act as Protector of the kingdom.

Nevertheless there were many, including Queen Marguerite, who were quite unprepared to accept this disinheritance of Prince Edward. Henry was obliged to sign an order summoning the Queen and Prince to London, but they avoided capture, eventually arriving at Harlech Castle on the west coast of Wales, probably in company with Jasper.

Sir William Herbert, who had now returned to the Yorkist party, together with his brother-in-law, Sir Walter Devereux the Younger, his half-brother Roger Vaughan and a number of others, were sent to capture Jasper. Marguerite had left Harlech for the north of England, where she succeed in raising another army which York now left London to try to defeat. Simultaneously, York's son, Edward, Earl of March, was heading for Wales in pursuit of Jasper. York was heavily defeated and killed at the Battle of Wakefield on 30th December 1460, together with Salisbury, and York's second son Edmund, Earl of Rutland (killed after the battle by Lord Clifford in revenge for his own father's death).

Following this, it was imperative for York's son, Edward of March, to prevent Marguerite's victorious Lancastrians from meeting up with Jasper's men.

Jasper was joined by James Butler, Earl of Wiltshire, a loyal Lancastrian although his personal courage was doubted as he had swiftly run away from the battlefield of St Albans. Jasper was also accompanied by his father, Owain, as well as by Thomas and Owain ap Gruffydd ap Nicolas. The two armies met at Mortimer's Cross just outside Hereford on 2nd (or possibly 3rd) February. Edward of March, who was victorious on every battlefield he commanded, won resoundingly.

Jasper escaped from battlefield but his father was not so lucky and he was executed in the market cross in Hereford. Apparently his last words expressed his amazement that the head which had once lain in Queen Katherine's lap was now to be placed on the block. Sir Roger Vaughan, in charge of the executions, ignored his pleas.

Edward turned back for London in an effort to reach the capital before Marguerite entered from the North. She had demolished another Yorkist army at St Albans on 16th February, reuniting with Henry VI who had been present, in Yorkist control, and was heading for the capital.

The Londoners, fearing what they had heard of the unruliness of the Lancastrian army had closed the gates to the Queen. In one of the few moments when Queen Marguerite's determination and ruthlessness failed her, she remained outside of the city to negotiate, rather than advancing. In the meantime Edward entered from the west and was proclaimed King.

Chapter 9: Exile

Jasper retreated to West Wales and sent letters to his supporters, urging them to be faithful to the cause of Lancaster and to help him avenge the death of his father, Owain. He was bitter against his former councillor, Sir William Herbert, and Sir Roger Vaughan, whom he saw as the murderer of his father.

The new King, Edward IV, was determined to extirpate all remnants of Lancastrian support. He marched north with all possible speed securing victory, first at Ferrybridge, and then on 29th March 1461 presided over the bloodiest battle ever fought on English soil when the Lancastrians were decimated at Towton. It is alleged that some 75,000 men fought and around 28,000 were killed. King Henry, Queen Marguerite and Prince Edward fled for Scotland. Jasper seems not to have fought at Towton but stayed in Wales maintaining his affinity, and holding Pembroke, Denbigh and Harlech castles for Henry VI.

Edward was crowned on 29th June and immediately proceeded to re-grant such of Jasper's estates as he could control to Sir William Herbert, now Lord Herbert of Raglan. In September, Herbert was granted custody of the states of the late Duke of Buckingham – the first Duke been killed at Northampton and the second at Towton whilst the latter's heir was still only a child.

A number of commissions were issued to Herbert and other Yorkist in South Wales to raise forces to capture Jasper. Pembroke was surrendered by Sir John Scudamore (son-in-law of Gruffydd ap Nicolas) who was eventually pardoned by Edward IV. The surrender of the castle brought Henry Tudor into Edward IV's hands and he was given in wardship to William Herbert, who paid £1000 for the privilege. Young Henry was still referred to as the Earl of Richmond, but his lands were confiscated and granted to the King's brother, George, Duke of Clarence.

The Lancastrian exiles in Scotland requested aid from Charles VI of France, Queen Marguerite's uncle (and Jasper's). She had asked him to send money and men to Jasper but before the embassy could reach the French court, King Charles died, to be replaced by Louis XI who at this point was inclined to favour the Yorkists and arrested Marguerite's messengers.

Jasper, from having been the King's dearly beloved half-brother and an important member of the government, was now a fugitive. His whereabouts are unknown but his castles of Denbigh, Carreg Cennen and Harlech held out as long as they could. Denbigh surrendered in January 1462 and Carreg Cennen in May 1462 whilst Harlech remained defiantly in Lancastrian hands under Dafydd ab Ieuan until 1468 – giving rise to that much loved Welsh song 'Men of Harlech'.

Jasper and the Duke of Exeter (Edward IV's brother-in-law) met Herbert in another skirmish at Twt Hill on the outskirts of Caernarfon in north-west Wales in October 1461. The Yorkists were again victorious but Jasper and Exeter escaped, heading for the Lancastrian court in exile in Scotland. On 4th November 1461 Jasper was attainted by Parliament as was his nephew, the four-year-old Henry Tudor.

Jasper's pre-eminence in Wales was now taken by Sir William Herbert (known as Gwilym Ddu, or Black Will, in Welsh). In due course, as well as receiving a number of new grants of land and titles from Edward IV, he was granted Jasper's earldom of Pembroke. Although Jasper and his brother Edmund had been the first Welshmen to receive the title of earl, Sir William was the first man of full Welsh descent to be so ennobled.

The continued resistance of Harlech remained a thorn in the side of Edward IV, offering the opportunity for Lancastrians to enter the country by sea, which in the 1460s lapped at its towers, to carry out raids.

Chapter 10: Resistance

In early 1462 Edward IV discovered plans for a Lancastrian invasion. The plan was allegedly for three separate forces to land - one in East Anglia, the second in Sandwich in Kent and a third in Wales. The coordinator in England, the Earl of Oxford, together with his son, Aubrey, was arrested, tried and executed. This left the earldom of Oxford in the hands of John de Vere who was confirmed in that title in 1464 by Edward IV but was later to revert to the Lancastrian allegiance. Jasper was, at the time, in Brittany requesting Breton support. He was joined there in April by Queen Marguerite, and together they travelled to the court of her father, René of Anjou, King of Naples, at Ardennes. King Rene was long on titles, but short on actual cash, and could do nothing to help his daughter and grandson.

Marguerite hoped that her cousin, Louis XI (who was also Jasper's cousin), would support Lancaster but Louis was not enthusiastic. Jasper made a flying visit to Henry VI, in Edinburgh, before being back in Normandy by 13th June and at the French court with Marguerite by the end of the month. The Queen had agreed a deal which must have made Louis XI rub his hands in glee. She had agreed that, in return for a loan of 20,000 livres tournois, she would mortgage Calais.

This was an act which lost Marguerite much of the support she had had in England – Calais was the last remnant of both the Angevin Empire of Henry II, and Henry V's conquest of France. Of course, in reality,

Calais was held by the Yorkist government, with Warwick still Captain and the likelihood of Louis ever getting his hands on it was slim. The agreement was enshrined in a treaty dated 28 June 1462, signed on behalf of Henry VI by Marguerite and also signed by Jasper.

In autumn of that year Jasper returned to Scotland to await the arrival of Marguerite and the French troops promised by Louis. Louis, however, was now under pressure from Edward IV and failed to provide as many troops as had been anticipated. The Lancastrians crossed the border into Northumberland and captured first Alnwick, then Bamburgh, Dunstanburgh and Warkworth castles.

Again the depredations of Margaret's troops (in this case largely Scottish and French) lost her local support. Various pockets of Lancastrians were besieged in these northern castles by Edward IV. Jasper tried to raise the siege of Bamburgh, but failed, although he did manage to enter into the castle. With no aid from Scotland or France forthcoming, Bamburgh was obliged to surrender on Christmas Eve 1462. The Duke of Somerset and Sir Ralph Percy accepted Edward IV's pardon and took an oath of allegiance to him. Jasper and Lord Roos declined to accept pardons, as Edward IV would not agree to restore their lands.

For some unaccountable reason Edward IV gave them safe conducts to return to Scotland, rather than taking the opportunity to imprison or execute them. Edward's motives for this are hard to understand – Jasper, unlike most of the rest of the English nobility, was not a relative of the King (at least only very distantly). It may have been Jasper's position as first cousin to the King of France that encouraged Edward to be lenient, or a desire to show himself in these early days as a King who could be trusted to keep his word.

In April of the following year, Jasper, together with Exeter and a number of other Lancastrians, left Scotland for the court of Burgundy. They were permitted to travel through Burgundian territory to the French court. In 1463, Marguerite and Prince Edward joined him there, whilst King Henry remained in Scotland under the care of the Bishop of St Andrews. Henry was later part of another Lancastrian force, heavily defeated, first at Hedgely Moor in April 1464, and, the following month at Hexham. After these defeats, Henry was a fugitive in northern England for over a year before being captured and imprisoned in the Tower of London.

Marguerite set up her court-in-exile in Bar, her father's duchy on the northern edge of France, which was part of the Holy Roman Empire, rather than a French fiefdom. It is probable that Jasper accompanied her.

Chapter 11: Fugitive

During the period 1463 to 1470, Jasper's exact whereabouts are difficult to pin down. He seems to have travelled between France, Bar, Brittany and Scotland, drumming up support for his half-brother and nephew. This activity led Edward IV to put pressure on Louis XI to extradite him. Louis would not go that far, but gave Jasper 500 livres tournois to depart his kingdom for Scotland in 1463. The following May, Louis furnished Jasper with a letter of recommendation for Duke François II of Brittany, requesting the Duke to help Jasper with troops and supplies to effect an invasion of Wales. François complied with Louis's request, but was then astonished to receive news from the French King that Louis was displeased about the aid granted to Jasper.

The position of France's neighbours, Brittany and Burgundy, is key to understanding the dynamics of the aid that was given at different times to both Lancaster and York. Henry VI was widely accepted as the legitimate King, and he initially had support from France, as the marriage alliance between Henry and Marguerite had been intended to end the Hundred Years' War. The Lancastrians had also been closely allied to Burgundy during the first half of the century. Charles of Burgundy, like Henry VI, was a great-grandson of John of Gaunt, and his aunt, Anne, had been married to Henry V's brother, John, Duke of Bedford. Brittany had been allied to the Lancastrian house through the marriage of Joanna of Navarre, grandmother of the current duke, to Henry IV.

However, France was looking to annex both Burgundy and Brittany. Charles of Burgundy had only a daughter, and, in the early 1460s, Francois of Brittany had no children at all. Thus, both Burgundy and Brittany sought allies to protect them from French incursions, whilst not wishing to provoke France into attack.

There are no definite records of where Jasper went in March 1464 with the money that Duke Francois had given him. It is possible that he landed in Wales, probably at Harlech, and he may have stayed at a place called Mostyn Hall.

Despite the apparent victory of Edward IV, all was not well in the Yorkist camp. Edward himself was a talented general, popular both with the public and with most of the nobility, once they had resigned themselves to the change of regime, which most did, following Towton. But he was becoming increasingly unpopular with the Earl of Warwick and his own brother, George, Duke of Clarence.

Warwick and Clarence felt they had not been sufficiently rewarded by Edward and Warwick was particularly displeased when his negotiations for Edward's marriage to Louis XI's sister-in-law, Bona of Savoy, collapsed on the news that Edward had already married in secret. Warwick felt himself to be a laughingstock – not an experience that such a proud man welcomed.

By 1468 Edward was facing dissatisfaction at home from his former supporters and had also provoked Louis XI through his alliances with Brittany and Burgundy. In 1468, Charles of Burgundy had married Margaret of York, Edward IV's sister. This did not immediately put Charles into the Yorkist camp, but it kept his options open, and gave him a potential ally against Louis XI.

In retaliation, on 1st June 1468, Louis furnished Jasper with three ships and nearly 300 livres tournois for an expedition to Wales. Obviously this was not sufficient for a full-scale invasion but was probably intended as reconnaissance trip. It's likely that Jasper landed somewhere near Harlech Castle. There were still plenty of Lancastrians in Wales and Jasper soon formed an army of around 2,000 men which he led to Denbigh. He did not attempt, on this occasion, to retake the castle but instead burned the town. He followed this up by holding several legal sessions in the name of King Henry – hoping to demonstrate that Henry was the legitimate King.

These actions of Jasper's stirred Edward IV to even greater efforts to reduce Harlech. Herbert and his kinsman, Ferrers, as Sir Walter Devereux, was now known, raised as many as 10,000 men in the Marches and ravaged the whole of Nantconwy, an area of North Wales still largely Lancastrian. A number of Jasper's men were captured and Herbert's men settled down in front of Harlech to besiege it with Jasper perhaps inside.

The castle eventually fell. The majority of the garrison was spared. Jasper himself escaped again, allegedly disguising himself as a peasant carrying a bale of straw. Herbert was rewarded on 8th September 1468 by the grant of Jasper's title of Earl of Pembroke.

Chapter 12: Yorkist Squabbling

In a further crack-down on Lancastrian sympathisers, the young Earl of Oxford was arrested and imprisoned in the Tower. Following his father and brother's execution, he had been allowed to inherit his title, and been created a Knight of the Bath for Elizabeth Woodville's coronation, but something gave rise to suspicion, and Edward took action. Oxford was pardoned in April 1469, but he soon joined the anti-Edward plot being fomented by his brother-in-law, Warwick, and the King's brother, Clarence.

Warwick and Clarence raised rebellion against Edward in June 1469. This was not initially with the purpose of restoring the Lancastrians, but rather with the aim of restoring Warwick's power and influence and permitting the marriage of Warwick's daughter to Clarence – a match forbidden by Edward IV. Warwick, Clarence and Oxford all left the country for Calais, to raise men.

On 15th July 1469 Warwick landed in Kent. In a confusing series of marches and counter-marches Edward's supporters, led by William Herbert, met Warwick and his men at Edgecote near Banbury. In the ensuing battle, Edward's army (he was not present himself) was heavily defeated and Herbert was killed.

Herbert had been accompanied by his ward, Henry Tudor, who at 13, was still too young to fight. The boy was led away from the battlefield either by one of Herbert's friends, Sir Richard Corbet, or by Herbert's brother-in-law, Ferrers. Whichever of the men it was, Henry was taken to the Devereux home at Weobley in Herefordshire. Whilst he was there, his mother, Lady Margaret Beaufort, whose husband Sir Henry Stafford had submitted to Edward IV after the battle of Towton, sent messages and money – including 20 shillings for bows and arrows for archery practice.

The Battle of Edgecote had cut a swathe through the ranks of Welsh Yorkists. Herbert had been a notable patron of traditional Welsh bardic culture, and there was an outpouring of poetry urging support for a leader who would avenge the death of their hero, Gwilym Ddu. It did not much matter whether that leader was a Yorkist or a Lancastrian. This was to stand Henry Tudor and Jasper in good stead in 1485.

Warwick was now in control and captured Edward IV before the latter could raise fresh troops. The King was obliged to go first to Warwick Castle, and then to Middleham, in Yorkshire. Unfortunately for the Earl, however, he was in no way able to rule the country without Edward's authority. The other Lords simply would not listen to him. As rioting and unrest increased throughout the country, Warwick was obliged to free King Edward on 10th September.

Edward agreed to pardon all of those who had been involved in the attempted coup, including both Warwick and Clarence. Edward was a shrewd man – always genial and charming, he avoided bloodshed unless there were positive gains to be had and he often gave rebels a second chance – although if he was pushed too far, he could be ruthless.

The King then led an army north to put down Lancastrian incursions there, before returning to London. To replace Herbert in Wales, Edward promoted his close friend, William, Lord Hastings, as Justiciar of North Wales and his younger brother, Richard, Duke of Gloucester, just 17 years old, to the office of Constable of England. He also granted him the

Earldom of March, the largest and most powerful of the Marcher lordships, covering much of the southern border between England and Wales.

There is no evidence of Jasper's location during this period of turmoil, but by October 1469 he was certainly at the court of Louis XI where he remained until September 1470, receiving a monthly pension of one hundred livres tournois.

Warwick and Clarence, having been forgiven for their treachery, seemed unable to leave well alone. Warwick was suspected of stirring up trouble in Lincolnshire between Lord Welles and Sir Thomas Burgh. Edward IV won a swift victory over Welles' men at Losecoat Field on 12th March and Welles implicated Warwick and Clarence in his illegal activities before being executed.

The jig was now up for Warwick. He and Clarence fled to Calais taking Warwick's daughter Isabel, who was Clarence's duchess, with them even though she was heavily pregnant and in fact she miscarried during in a storm in the Channel.

Chapter 13: Readeption of Henry VI

On 1st May, Warwick and Clarence, swiftly followed by Oxford, were welcomed with open arms by Jasper who now sought, together with Louis XI, to affect a reconciliation between Queen Marguerite and her former enemy. Jasper remained completely devoted to the Lancastrian cause – obviously aware that Henry VI would never again be an effective King, it was his aim to ensure that his nephew, Edward of Lancaster, was crowned as King.

Eventually Marguerite was induced to put her trust in Warwick. In recognition of the rapprochement, Edward of Lancaster was married to Warwick's younger daughter, Anne Neville. This gave Warwick a daughter in both the Lancastrian camp and also potentially in the Yorkist camp should Clarence succeed Edward IV as the Yorkist heir (at this time Edward IV had no sons). One story is that Warwick was kept on his knees for fifteen minutes to alleviate Marguerite's anger against him for the many losses she had suffered. Other accounts show her as more pragmatic and receiving him graciously. It was agreed that Jasper and Warwick were to lead an initial invasion, to be followed up by Marguerite and Prince Edward, together with his new bride. As a sop to Clarence he was recognised as heir to his new brother-in-law Prince Edward.

On 9th September 1470, Jasper, together with Oxford, Warwick and Clarence, sailed from Normandy. Jasper had been confirmed in his title of Earl of Pembroke and was appointed as joint Lieutenant with Prince Edward for Henry VI. The little fleet landed on 13th September, first at Dartmouth and then Plymouth. Some accounts say that the move from Dartmouth to Plymouth was because of a poor reception in the first town. The leaders then separated. Jasper headed for Wales, where he could be sure of support, and Warwick for London. Disturbances had been organised in the north to lure Edward away from the capital.

Edward was completely outmanoeuvred when Warwick's brother, Montague, previously a committed Yorkist, defected. Suddenly surrounded by enemies, Edward immediately took ship for Burgundy, together with his younger brother, Richard of Gloucester. There they threw themselves on the mercy of their brother-in-law Charles, Duke of Burgundy, who initially greeted them very coldly.

Warwick, having reached the capital, freed Henry VI from his captivity in the Tower of London. Henry who appeared dazed, unkempt and hardly a fine figure of a King, was re-crowned to wash away the stains of his deposition. The risk of Marguerite's alliance with Louis XI was now exposed as Warwick, in accordance with the agreement made with the French king, was obliged to declare war on Burgundy. This move changed Charles of Burgundy from a mildly supportive Lancastrian to a willing supporter of Edward of York.

Jasper was now reunited with his nephew, Henry Tudor, whom he collected from the Devereux estates, and with the boy's mother, his other sister-in-law, Lady Margaret Beaufort. Jasper was in the interesting position of being uncle both to the nearest Lancastrian heir, Edward Prince of Wales, and of the more distant Lancastrian, Henry Tudor.

Jasper and Henry Tudor spent a week or so with Margaret and her husband, Stafford, at their home at Woking before heading west.

Together with Warwick, Jasper was now the most powerful man in England, exercising his role as Henry VI's Lieutenant. The Parliament called in December 1470 repealed the legislation of Edward IV's reign and restored Jasper to the position he had held before Edward's coronation in 1461. This, of course, included the earldom of Pembroke. Rather confusingly, as Herbert's son had never been attainted by Parliament, he also was technically Earl of Pembroke. Jasper received new grants, including the wardship of the minor son of Lord Grey of Powys which gave him control of significant lands in the Welsh Marches and some of the lands of the young Duke of Buckingham, who had been moved to the Yorkist affinity, when he was married to Katherine Woodville, sister of Edward IV's queen.

Chapter 14: Resurgence of Edward IV

Edward of York was not content to lose his throne. In early 1471, he was supplied with a small flotilla by Charles of Burgundy and made for the English coast. There were sufficient Lancastrian forces in East Anglia to prevent his landing there, but he arrived more or less unopposed at Ravenspur in Yorkshire. Whilst he did not have a huge following, the city of York was persuaded to allow him to enter when he claimed that he sought only to have his dukedom of York reinstated.

Clarence now realised that he had no hope of becoming King and presumably decided that it was better to play second fiddle to his brother Edward IV than to his brother-in-law Edward of Lancaster. He therefore re-joined his brother. Edward marched south, gathering support en-route and entered London unopposed on 11th April. He had always enjoyed the support of London and he immediately took control of government, dispatching Henry VI to the Tower once more.

Oxford, together with Warwick, brought their troops to Barnet just north of London. Unfortunately for the Lancastrians, owing to the similarity between Oxford's banner of the star and that of Edward's sun-in-splendour, there was confusion amongst the troops and the Lancastrian centre fired on Oxford's men. Oxford believing that this was treachery on the part of Warwick, left the field taking the remainder of his troops with him. Both Warwick and his brother, Montague, were killed. Amongst the Yorkist army was Henry Stafford, husband of Lady Margaret Beaufort. Although he had been requested to send troops to the Duke of Somerset's Lancastrian force he had decided to continue his allegiance to Edward.

Following the Battle of Barnet, Oxford and Somerset headed south west to meet with Marguerite, Edward of Lancaster, his wife, Anne

Neville, and Anne's mother, the Countess of Warwick, who had arrived from France. They had landed at Weymouth and had been met by a number of Lancastrian supporters including Dr John Morton, who later played a significant role in the ultimate victory of Henry VII.

Marguerite and her entourage headed for Cerne Abbey and it was there, on 15th April, that she heard of the defeat at Barnet. Her immediate reaction was to return to France but Jasper and the other Lancastrian lords, Wenlock, Somerset, Devon and Dorset, as well as her own son, persuaded Marguerite that they should fight. Jasper travelled swiftly to Wales to begin raising troops, whilst the remnants of the Lancastrian troops from Barnet joined Marguerite's force.

Edward of York, who had re-entered London, soon heard of the Lancastrian plans. Unsure as to whether Marguerite's intention was to march west to join with Jasper or to move straight for London, Edward headed for Cirencester, which he reached on 29th April. It soon became apparent that the Lancastrians were heading for the Severn crossing to meet Jasper, and probably gain recruits from Cheshire.

Somerset and his men had been welcomed at Bristol, but the city of Gloucester, receiving urgent messages from Edward, closed its gates to the Lancastrian forces who, having undertaken a night march of 36 miles were thus forced to continue to the next crossing point on the Severn at Tewkesbury a further 24 miles, an astonishing feat of endurance. It was matched only by the march of Edward's men from Sodbury Hill to Tewkesbury, so quickly that the Lancastrians had no time to cross the river.

The Lancastrians had no option but to fight with the army they had. Marguerite herself went on to the battlefield to encourage her troops before retiring with the other women to a nearby manor house. Young Edward of Lancaster was present at his first battle – which also proved to be his last, when the Lancastrians were annihilated. There are differing accounts of whether Edward of Lancaster was killed in the battle or whether he was executed in cold blood by Edward IV and his brothers, Clarence and the 18 year old Richard of Gloucester after the battle. The other Lancastrian leaders who had sought sanctuary in Tewkesbury were forced out, and executed on the orders of Gloucester, using his authority as Constable of England.

Chapter 15: The End of Lancaster?

For Marguerite the war was now over. Her son was dead and within a few days she heard that her husband too was dead, almost certainly killed in the Tower on the orders of Edward IV. The Queen was gathered up with the other women and sent to London, following which she spent four bitter years of humiliation in captivity, before being ransomed by Louis XI. For Jasper, however, all was not lost. He was still at large in Chepstow.

Edward sent Sir Roger Vaughan, Jasper's old enemy, to capture him. Getting wind of Vaughan's approach, Jasper's men captured him and he was executed on Jasper's orders, apparently saying he would show Vaughan as much mercy as Vaughan had shown to Owain Tudor after Mortimer's Cross.

Jasper still had in his hands his nephew, Henry Tudor, who was now a possible heir of the Lancastrian claim to the throne although it seems unlikely that, with Edward now firmly seated on the throne anyone believed there was any realistic prospect of Henry Tudor taking up the Lancastrian mantle. Nevertheless, Jasper allegedly received urgent messages from Henry's mother, Margaret Beaufort, to keep her son out of Edward's hands. A more likely Lancastrian heir was Henry Holland, Duke of Exeter, who, badly wounded at Barnet, had been captured by Edward IV.

Exeter was Edward's brother-in-law, which may have inclined Edward to spare his life, although he and Anne of York hated each other, and the marriage was annulled the following year. Exeter himself died in somewhat mysterious circumstances in 1475, apparently reconciled to Edward but unaccountably falling overboard when returning from France with Edward's army after a military expedition. Another possible heir was Henry Stafford, Duke of Buckingham, although as his claim derived from the last of Edward III's sons, it was inferior to that of both York and Lancaster.

By early May 1471 Jasper and Henry were at Pembroke Castle, obviously intending to escape by sea. The castle was quickly surrounded by Edward's men, led by Morgan ap Thomas, a grandson of Gruffydd ap Nicolas. Morgan's brother, Dafydd ap Thomas, continuing his father's and grandfather's tradition of loyalty to Jasper, approached Morgan's army from the rear to raise the siege and ferry Jasper and Henry to Tenby. It is, of course, perfectly possible that Morgan had not been terribly enthusiastic in his activities and that the brothers had concocted the scheme together to keep the family in favour with both sides.

Jasper and Henry, now 14, remained in hiding in Tenby for a few days until a ship could be found to take them to France.

It had been Jasper's intention to return to the court of Louis XI, who would almost certainly have given him support in the face of Edward IV's belligerent attitude toward France. However the ship was blown off-course and the two men arrived instead in Brittany. Duke François II, who is one of the few men who comes out of the Wars of the Roses with any honour, permitted them to remain in Brittany.

He treated them well, and kept the promises he made that, so long as they remained in his territories, they would be *'far from injury'*. Nevertheless the men were political prisoners. François still had no heir (he would eventually have a daughter, Anne, in 1477, but that was not much better than no heir at all, in the face of French aggression) and he need every bargaining tool he could find.

Edward IV, as soon as he became aware of the whereabouts of the two Tudors, requested that Duke François extradite them. François refused. He stated that he had given his word to the Tudors that they would be safe and he could not break his vow. He would, however, ensure that they could not do Edward IV any harm.

Chapter 16: European Politics

Initially Jasper and Henry were kept together, first at the Chateau de l'Hermine near Vannes, and then at Suscinio, a location further from the coast. Both Edward IV and Louis XI demanded that François keep the Tudors less as guests and more as prisoners. The former because he was concerned lest they foment further Lancastrian rebellions and the latter nervous that Edward IV might find means to capture or kill them. So, in order to maximise his negotiating power, François decided to separate Jasper and his nephew. Jasper was sent to the fortress of Josselin and Henry to Largoet.

Jasper's personal attendants were dismissed and replaced with Bretons. It is interesting to speculate on how well Jasper may have been able to communicate with the Bretons whose language was (and is) very similar to Welsh. It is unlikely that Jasper spoke Welsh as a first language, having been brought up at Barking Abbey where he would have learnt English and French, however it is likely that he knew some Welsh. He had spent significant amounts of time in Wales and that would certainly have been the language of his father. It is therefore probable that Jasper would have been able to communicate with his Breton retinue. Henry too, although we do not know for certain his linguistic abilities, had spent the first 14 years of his life in Wales – first at Pembroke and then at Raglan where Herbert kept a traditional Welsh court. It is extremely likely that he understood Welsh and probably spoke it to a greater or lesser degree. In later life, Henry showed a marked preference for speaking French.

Meanwhile, that other committed Lancastrian, the Earl of Oxford, was still causing trouble for Edward IV. Funded by Louis XI, he collected a fleet of about a dozen ships and undertook raids on Calais and St Osyth in Essex. In late 1473 he captured St Michael's Mount in Cornwall which he held for some eight months. Eventually captured, he was not executed but sent to perpetual imprisonment at the Castle of Hammes near Calais, together with the other Lancastrian leader, Lord Beaumont.

Whilst Jasper and Henry were confined in their separate keeps, the political landscape outside was changing. Edward IV raised an enormous army, at great cost, with a view to reconquering France, in which he was to be aided by his brother-in-law, Charles of Burgundy. The strategy was exactly that which Henry V had had sixty years earlier, but, instead of an insane king and a nobility riven by strife, France was now led by the exceptionally astute Louis. It is not for nothing that he gained the epithet the '*spider*' King – a reference to his ability to patiently weave webs of intrigue.

Louis undermined the Anglo-Burgundian alliance by financing a large Swiss mercenary army to distract Charles on his eastern borders. Edward's troops were permitted to pass through Burgundy, but not to enter any of the towns as Charles, not surprisingly, was worried about the depredations that foreign troops might impose on his people. Louis had carefully refrained from giving battle and Edward was now in a position where he was running short of supplies, winter was approaching and it was difficult for him to realistically achieve his objectives.

It also been suggested, initially by Louis's own minister, Philip de Commynes, that Edward, having won his throne, had lost interest in military prowess, preferring to spend his time indulging in the pleasures of the flesh. Louis made an offer to Edward that the latter found he could not refuse. A one-off payment of 75,000 crowns and an annual pension of 50,000. This was agreed at the Treaty of Picquiny, signed on 29th August. Louis, knowing he had more than one man to persuade, gave plump presents to the vast majority of Edward's Council.

This agreement somewhat tarnished Edward's prestige abroad as military commander – it was seen as a dishonourable outcome. Back in England, Parliament was displeased that it had raised money and men for no apparent gain – obviously, Edward was not going to pay back the taxes raised. Those lords who were beneath the notice of the King of France and had not received bribes, were disgruntled because they had no opportunity of gathering plunder or ransoms.

Charles of Burgundy was still fighting the Swiss and he was killed on 5th January 1477 at the Battle of Nancy. He was succeeded in those parts of his territories which would accept female rule, by his daughter Mary, now Duchess of Burgundy. However a large part of Burgundy, the hereditary lands of the French crown, reverted to Louis. The King of France was now stronger than any of his ancestors had been.

Chapter 17: The Long Exile

This resurgence of France gave François of Brittany something of a headache. His Burgundian ally was now weak and France was freed from the threat of invasion from England for at least seven years. As part of the treaty Edward had extracted a promise from Louis that François would be left in peace. In return for this, Edward suggested that François might like to hand over the Tudors as evidence of his gratitude.

In order to sweeten any smell of betrayal, Edward added that his main reason for wanting Henry Tudor to be sent back to England was for him to be married to one of Edward's daughters. The young man would receive not just a bride but would also be confirmed in his Beaufort inheritance.

Persuaded by this mixture of conciliation and advice from his Council, many of whom had received 'presents' from Edward, François decided that he would send the young Earl of Richmond to England. Henry had previously refused to return with Edward's envoys.

In November 1476 Henry, dragging his feet, was taken to Vannes where he was handed over to Edward's messengers who planned to take ship at St Malo. Whilst the party were waiting for a favourable tide, one of Duke François' most important councillors, who had been absent from the earlier discussions, raced to the Duke's court and pleaded with him to change his mind, assuring François that if Henry were handed over he would be *'torn in pieces by bloodied butchers...miserably tormented and finally... slain.'*

François, persuaded that he should not have gone back on his word, sent his minister, Pierre Landais, to St Malo to fetch Henry back. Henry, meanwhile was suffering from a severe fever either genuine, feigned or brought on by fear and stress. Whilst Landais was demanding that Henry be returned to François, Henry slipped from his sick bed and took refuge in the Cathedral of Saint Vincent.

The populace prevented the angry English messengers from breaking sanctuary and they were forced to return home empty-handed. There is no record of whether Jasper was with Henry although it seems reasonable to suppose that Edward would have wanted to lay his hands on both of them. They are next found together back at the court of François, before again being separated and kept in somewhat stricter confinement than previously, as a sop to Edward IV.

Louis XI to was still trying to get hold of the Tudors and sent money to Duke François in both 1477 and 1482 in a bid to persuade him to release them to the French court, but François refused. By 1482 the two men had been reunited and were in the care of François' chief councillor, Jean de Robihan.

Further temptation to hand over uncle and nephew was placed in François' way in 1482 when Edward promised him a contingent of archers to defend Brittany's borders if the Tudors were extradited. Negotiations were interrupted by Edward's sudden death in April 1483.

François had promised Edward that Jasper and Henry would not be able to do him any harm but once the King was dead, he was released from that promise and could give the men more freedom. Astonishing events now unfolded in England, which took Henry Tudor from being a minor irritation under the Yorkist saddle to being a serious contender for the throne, not just as a Lancastrian but as a focal point for Yorkists who were horrified at the usurpation of the throne by Richard III from Edward's sons.

Chapter 18: Buckingham's Rebellion

In August 1483, François sent a messenger, Georges de Manbier, to negotiate with Richard III. He told Richard that Louis XI was threatening to invade Brittany if Henry were not handed over. Richard and Louis were not on good terms as Richard had refused Louis' bribes at the time of the Treaty of Picquiny. Richard could be sure that Louis would use Henry Tudor as a weapon against him.

In return for François holding onto the Tudors, he would need Richard to supply him not only with the archers previously promised by Edward IV, but another 2,000 to 3,000 men to protect Brittany from France. These terms were extremely high, and Richard had little chance of meeting them. It is unlikely that François was sincere in his negotiations as he was already backing the invasion that the Tudors undertook in the late summer of 1483 as part of a wider rebellion against Richard, known as Buckingham's Rebellion.

Jasper and Henry were lent five ships manned by 320 or so men and 10,000 crowns in cash by the Duke, together with a promise of a further 5,000 men. Although Henry and Jasper arrived in England, they were too late to join Buckingham's rebellion which had been easily suppressed by Richard III. Rather than landing they turned round immediately and headed back for Brittany. Owing to the vagaries of tides and weather, they landed on the coast of France but were granted safe conduct to pass into Brittany.

This failure to capitalise on the Tudors landing in France occurred because Louis XI had died leaving a minor son, Charles VIII, and a Regency government, led by Charles' sister, Anne of Beaujeu. Back in the city of Vannes, Henry was joined by increasing numbers of senior Yorkists, including Queen Elizabeth Woodville's son, the Marquess of

Dorset, her brother, Sir Edward Woodville, and a number of West Country gentlemen - the Courtenays, Sir Giles Daubeny and Sir Richard Edgecombe.

Henry swore an oath in the Cathedral at Rennes, that, once he became King of England, he would marry Elizabeth of York or, if she were unavailable, one of her sisters, and unite the Lancastrian and Yorkist factions. He was promised support by Duke François and his councillor, Pierre Landais.

Back in England the Parliament that opened in January 1484 passed Acts of Attainder against the Earl of Oxford, Jasper, Henry and Henry's mother, Lady Margaret Beaufort, who was now married to Thomas, Lord Stanley, who had been a loyal supporter of Edward IV.

Soon after this, the political landscape in Brittany changed again as François II fell ill and his councillors were divided between those who wanted to ally with England and those who saw an opportunity for alliance with unruly French nobles, such as Louis of Orleans. Richard III kept up the pressure by seizing Breton shipping and goods. He promised to desist and even to grant the income from the lands of the exiles, if François were to hand the Tudors over. François was seriously ill and government was now in the hands of Landais, who agreed that Jasper and Henry would be handed over, in exchange for England's support against France.

Jasper and Henry got wind of the plot and swiftly sent a request to Anne of Beaujeu to admit them to France. The two men separated, Jasper taking a group of followers to visit François on his sickbed, conveniently close to the French border. Rather than visiting the Duke, Jasper crossed the border and headed for the city of Anjou. A couple of days after Jasper had left Vannes, Henry taking a retinue of only five men, set out, ostensibly to visit a friend. Having ridden five miles, the party disappeared into a forest where Henry changed clothes with one of his servants and with just one other man, rode as fast as he could for the border, crossing it just an hour before Landais' men arrived. François, discovering the treachery of his councillor, gave large gifts of money to Henry's followers and permitted them to cross into France, covering their expenses. Landais ended on a gibbet.

Chapter 19: Planning Invasion

Charles VIII and Anne of Beaujeu welcomed their cousins with open arms. They were fed, housed, given money to pay their men and given permission to raise troops to effect an invasion of England. Soon, they were joined by Oxford and Beaumont, who had escaped from imprisonment, largely by persuading their gaoler, Sir James Blount, to join Henry's growing band of supporters.

It became apparent to Richard III that he would have to fight for his Crown and soon - Henry could not afford to delay. The ever-changing politics of France and Brittany meant that at any time he might be handed over to Richard in return for support. Nevertheless prospects for the little Lancastrian court-in-exile looked good as increasing numbers of disaffected Yorkists were either leaving England or sending messages of support. According to Henry's first biographer, Polydor Vergil, one of these messages came from Rhys ap Thomas in South Wales. Following the death of Herbert, Rhys at Thomas was one of the most powerful influences in south-west and west Wales. Without his support it would be difficult for Henry to make a landing in that locality.

On 4th May 1485 the French Parliament agreed to lend 40,000 livres tournois for an invasion fleet. Uncle and nephew set up their headquarters in Rouen and wrote copious letters to England requesting support, including to William Herbert's son, another William, promising that should Henry be unable to marry one of Edward IV's daughters, he would marry William's sister, Katherine. William and Katherine Herbert were both well known to Henry as he had spent his childhood in their home. The third sibling, Maud, who had once been suggested as a wife for Henry by her father, was now married to Henry Percy, Earl of Northumberland. Northumberland, too, had once been a ward of Herberts, at Raglan with Henry Tudor. These boyhood good relationship may have influenced first Herbert and then Northumberland's actions at the Battle of Bosworth.

From this point forward Jasper is overshadowed by his nephew. Whilst it is apparent from the poetry and prophesyings of the Welsh bards of the period, that Jasper was in communication with men in Wales and that the Tudors were assured of a warm welcome, the language of these effusions is not sufficiently precise to give a detailed history of events.

Henry, accompanied by Jasper, landed near Milford Haven on 7th August sporting the Welsh Dragon of the mythical ancient British king, Cadwallader, as well as the red cross of St George on his banners. The Tudor forces quickly moved through south Wales, keeping to the west coast and headed for Aberystwyth. The Herberts did nothing to prevent their advance but neither did Rhys Thomas immediately fulfil any promise that might have been made to support Henry. Jasper, of course, may well have been nervous about the Herberts' intentions, having beheaded their kinsman, Roger Vaughan.

As Henry and Jasper travelled north they heard that Rhys Thomas and Sir Walter Herbert were marching parallel to them up the valley of the Teifi. The Tudors cannot have known whether these men were intending to join their ranks or cut them off at the knees. Fortunately, it was the former. With these increased numbers, Henry's march continued through Wales and he crossed into England at Shrewsbury, meeting Richard III at the Battle of Bosworth on 22nd August 1485.

Curiously, there is no definite record of Jasper's presence at Bosworth but it seems highly likely that he was present and he is referred to in some later poetry as positioned, together with Henry, in the centre section of the Tudor force. The man in overall charge of military arrangements was the Earl of Oxford.

Chapter 20: Reward & Retirement

Henry's strategy was one of reconciliation. He had never lived in England and the only nobles he knew, other than the Herberts and the Duke of Northumberland, were those who had joined him in Brittany. He therefore did not have the personal likes and dislikes that had so influenced the Wars of the Roses. Whilst he was eager to reward his supporters appropriately, he did not wish to indulge in wholesale revenge against Yorkists, nor to create new over-mighty subjects, such as York and Warwick had been. General pardons were issued and a policy of forgive and forget was the order of the day.

Jasper was by far the most generously rewarded of Henry supporters. On 20th October, having already been reconfirmed as Earl of Pembroke, he was created Duke of Bedford. The only other dukedoms that Henry was to create were for his sons. The choice of the title of Bedford was probably intended as a reference to Henry V's faithful brother, John of Lancaster, Duke of Bedford, who had valiantly tried to maintain English rule in France during the youth of Henry VI. It was undoubtedly intended as a mark of Jasper's proximity to the House of Lancaster.

The ceremony took place at Westminster Palace. The new Duke was led to the throne to kneel in front of the King by the Duke of Suffolk, brother-in-law to Edward IV and Richard III, and his son, John de la Pole, Earl of Lincoln. In a strange irony, the Duke of Suffolk had once been the infant husband of Henry's mother, Margaret Beaufort. Jasper also received the position of Chief Justice of South Wales and the Marcher Lordship of South Glamorgan, previously in the hands of the Earl of Warwick.

In a further display of Henry's affection for his uncle, Jasper was granted the honour of carrying the King's Crown in the Coronation procession and was later appointed as Lord High Steward at the coronation of Elizabeth of York

Jasper not only received lands and titles, including Sudeley Castle, he also, for the first time in his life was given a wife. It is not clear why he had not married during the early 1450s at the same time as his brother Edmund. To remain unmarried at the age of around 54, Jasper's current age, was extremely unusual. There are later accounts of a couple of illegitimate children but there were no rumours of any at the time nor any evidence from his accounts that he had any children.

The wife selected for the new duke was Katherine Woodville, younger sister of Queen Elizabeth Woodville, and the widow of Henry, 2nd Duke of Buckingham. It was notorious that, despite having been married in their youth, Buckingham and Katherine had lived on very bad terms – apparently he resented being married to somebody he considered unworthy of his Royal blood. Despite this, they had managed to produce four children, including Edward, now 3rd Duke (later executed by Henry VIII).

The marriage of Jasper and Katherine was one of the series of marriages that was intended to bring the warring factions of Lancaster and York together. Henry himself married Elizabeth of York as promised, his mother's nephew, Sir Richard Pole, married Margaret of Clarence, and Cicely of York married Lord Welles, who was Margaret Beaufort's stepbrother.

The marriage to Katherine enabled Henry VII to improve Jasper's lot financially without having to alienate Crown lands. Katherine was granted a very extensive dower from Buckingham estates comprising some 35 lordships across the whole of South Wales and in the south and midlands of England, although the wardship of the young Duke was given to Lady Margaret Beaufort. Parliament also confirmed his title to everything that had been granted to Jasper by Henry VI, although, in practical terms, not all of the lands could be recovered. Pembroke Castle, however, was returned to Jasper, who made some improvements there, including a more modern lodging for domestic use. Katherine and Jasper had no children.

Jasper was at the heart of Henry's government for the first few years, named as Privy Councillor, Lieutenant of Calais and titular Deputy of Ireland (a role held in reality by the Earl of Kildare). Rather grandly for a man who had spent much of his life fleeing pursuing armies, he was announced by heralds as *'the high and mighty prince, Jasper, brother and uncle of kings, Duke of Bedford and Earl of Pembroke'.*

In 1486 - 87, Jasper performed further military duties. A remnant of Yorkist supporters were resisting Henry's authority, under the command of Richard III's friend, Francis, Lord Lovell. Jasper travelled north, armed not only with men, but also with pardons for any rebels who would submit to the King, and, handily, a bull of excommunication from the Pope for any who persisted in rebellion. The tactics were effective and the rebellion faded away. Jasper was then called to Wales, where, together with Sir Rhys ap Thomas, he suppressed rebellion by Thomas Vaughan, son of the man Jasper had executed for killing his own father. No further reprisals were taken, however, and Vaughan was pardoned.

A more serious rebellion threatened, in the shape of a plot to put forward a pretender, Lambert Simnel, who had been crowned in Dublin as Edward VI. Presumably the Yorkists intended to replace him with the Earl of Lincoln when they had defeated Henry. Jasper, as Earl Marshal, had the job of gathering men for the King's army. Battle was finally joined at Stoke in Staffordshire with Jasper commanding the centre section, the King the rear section and Oxford and Rhys ap Thomas in the vanguard. Thus Jasper was one of the few men who was probably present both at the first battle of the Wars of the Roses, at St Albans, and also at the last. The royal army proved victorious.

But Jaspar's military career was not yet finished. In 1492, Henry invaded France, partly to protect the Duchy of Brittany, now in the hands of François' young daughter, Anne, who was being pressed to marry Charles VIII. Jasper and Oxford were again his chief commanders. Henry is not generally thought of as a military king but he was victorious in the two battles in which he fought – Bosworth and Stoke, and gave every indication that he would have pursued a campaign in France thoroughly and diligently. Hostilities opened with the English army besieging Boulogne. Charles VIII, keen to pursue his far more exciting claims in Italy than to get involved in a muddy campaign in northern France copied Louis XI's trick of buying off the English King. Henry departed with a pension of 50,000 crowns and the promise that the rebel Perkin Warbeck could no longer receive succour from the French.

Retirement

From around the end of 1480s, Jasper seemed to spend less time at court but he was appointed as deputy to Henry's new son, Arthur Prince of Wales, in 1491 and he and Arthur had a joint commission in 1493 to execute justice throughout Wales and the marches.

In December 1495 Jasper made his will. The vast majority of his lands were left to his nephew, excepting those which had been entailed on his great-nephew Henry, Duke of York (later Henry VIII). In common with the usual practice, there was significant sums bequeathed for prayers for his own soul, those of his parents and for his brother Edmund – dead for forty years, but obviously not forgotten. He was attended on his deathbed on 21st December by his wife, Katherine, Henry VII, Margaret Beaufort, and possibly Elizabeth of York.

Perhaps surprisingly, Jasper did not choose to be buried either in Wales with his brother Edmund, nor in Hereford with his father, but at Keynsham Abbey in Somerset which he had acquired only the year before.

Jasper's courage, self-sacrifice and devotion to his half-brother, his sisters-in-law, and his nephews is one of the outstanding examples of loyalty in an age when many changed coats more than once.

Part 2: Aspects of Jasper Tudor's Life

Chapter 21: Following the Footsteps of Jasper Tudor

Jasper Tudor must have covered more miles than almost any other protagonist of the Wars of the Roses. From the time he became an adult, until not long before his death, he was constantly on the move.

Granted enormous estates in south-west Wales by his half-brother, Henry VI, Jasper spent considerable time and money on improving the castle at Pembroke, and the fortifications at Tenby. Yet, owing to the dire political situation, he was obliged to travel extensively across the country – fighting battles, fleeing pursuers, and besieging Yorkist castles. He seems to have been a master of the secret escape – even dressing as a peasant carrying a bale of straw once!

The numbers in the article below correspond to those on the map which follows.

*

Life began quietly enough, at the Palace of Bishops Hatfield (1), a house owned by the Bishop of Ely, located about 30 miles north of London. The house that Jasper was born in was demolished and replaced in the 1480s by Bishop John Morton. The Great Hall of Morton's house is still standing, but the majority of his palace was replaced in the early 17th century by the fabulous Hatfield House, built by Sir Robert Cecil, Earl of Salisbury, and still occupied by his descendants.

The house and gardens are open to the public and are easily accessible by train from London.

Jasper's mother, Katherine de Valois, died when he was no more than five years old, and he was put in the care of the Abbess of Barking Abbey (2). Barking, in Essex, and now in east London, was one of the most important Benedictine convents in England, with the abbess taking precedence over all other abbesses and holding lands of the abbey from the king as a barony. It was one of the wealthiest abbeys and was frequently patronised by royal and noble widows wishing to retire from the world yet live in comfort. It is unlikely that Jasper would have endured any kind of monastic penury – the Abbess, Katherine de la Pole, was the sister of Henry VI's chief minister, the Earl of Suffolk, and she would have been expected to care for the King's half-brothers and bring them up as noblemen.

In 1443 it seems that the boys left Barking – it would be unsuitable for adolescent males to be housed amongst nuns. For the next nine years their specific location is unknown, but they were probably attached to court, and Henry VI is recorded as having taken great care that they should be brought up as pious and God-fearing men. Henry VI has had a reputation for piety and chastity – indeed, it took seven years for his wife to conceive – probably because of Henry's lack of enthusiasm for performing his marital duties. Henry VI's early biographer, John Blacman claimed that he was equally keen to ensure his half-brothers were chaste – perhaps this explains why Jasper's name was never linked with that of any woman before he married in his early fifties. Later stories of two illegitimate daughters are not reflected in contemporary records.

In 1453 Jasper was granted the earldom of Pembroke, the chief lands of which were in the far west of Wales, surrounding the enormous Pembroke Castle (3).

Pembroke Castle, situated overlooking the estuary of the River Cleddau, is a Norman castle. The first construction was begun in the 1090s by Arnulf de Montgomery, one of the barons of William the Conqueror. The early Normans had little interest in attempting to conquer upland Wales, but they were eager to take control of the southern and south-western coasts, in order to give them passage to Ireland. The castle was extensively strengthened and increased in size by William Marshall (c. 1147 – 1219), first Earl of Pembroke.

Jasper, too, spent time and money on enhancing Pembroke. Its location in the centre of the south-west peninsula of Wales makes it ideal for protecting both the River Cleddau, with its deep and sheltered natural harbour and the Bristol Channel. It was to Pembroke Castle that Jasper's sister-in-law, Lady Margaret Beaufort, Countess of Richmond, retired, aged only thirteen, to have her baby, following the deaths of Jasper's brother, Edmund. Pembroke Castle today is largely preserved and is open to the public.

As well as the extensive lands he was granted, Jasper's closeness to the King and Queen was probably the reason for another mark of favour - he was granted a tower in the Palace of Westminster (4) for life, as a place to hold his Councils and store his documents.

Pembroke Castle wasn't Jasper's only building project in the late 1450s. He entered into an agreement with the burgesses and town of Tenby (5), one of the other towns in his control as Earl of Pembroke. The town was to pay for half of the fortification of the town and improvements to its walls, whilst Jasper funded the other half. The walls were to be at least 6 foot wide, to give a sufficient platform for defenders.

Jasper then made over ownership of the walls to the town. Significant proportions of the town walls of Tenby are still visible today, and it is also worth visiting the Tudor Merchant's house, dating from 15th century, in the hands of the National Trust.

There has been some speculation over whether Jasper received the ordinary military training of a man of the English nobility. Whether or not he did receive formal training, he certainly seems to have understood military strategy and to have been an effective commander. In early 1460, Henry VI's government appointed Jasper as Constable for life of Denbigh Castle (6).

Denbigh, the enormous ruins of which are still visible, is one of the castles constructed by Edward I, following his annexation of Wales in the 1280s. Edward also created a Marcher Lordship, centred on Denbigh. The Marcher Lordships were jurisdictionally different from lands in England proper. In effect the Marcher Lords were petty kings – owing allegiance to the English Crown, but having jurisdictional rights within the Lordship. The earldom of Pembroke was also a one of them.

The Lordship of Denbigh had been inherited by Richard, Duke of York, as part of his Mortimer inheritance, and therefore the castle was garrisoned by his men. As York had been sent to Ireland as Lord Lieutenant with the objective of keeping him out of the country for as long as possible, the government wanted to prevent an easy return, via Denbigh on the North Wales coast.

Jasper was therefore required to take control of castle and the town. In order to do this effectively, he needed royal authority. He requested the King to give him permission to raise troops, to pardon any of York's garrison who submitted to him, and to take the goods and chattels of any of the garrison who resisted, to pay his troops. By May 1460, Jasper had achieved something that no previous commander had achieved – the capture of Denbigh. Even the great Welsh hero, Owain Glyndwr had been unable to besiege it successfully.

Unfortunately, Jasper's efforts proved to have been in vain. York did return to England, and although he was defeated and killed at the Battle of Wakefield, his son, Edward, Earl of March, was determined to prevent Jasper's forces from meeting with Queen Marguerite's army. In the first pitched battle where Jasper commanded men, he was unfortunate in facing Edward, who won every battle he fought. Jasper's force was heavily defeated at Mortimer's Cross (8), somewhere on the outskirts of Hereford.

The exact location of the battle has not been established, although it was on the route of the old London to Aberystwyth road which disappeared in the eighteenth century. The casualties at Mortimer's Cross were high, and not confined to the battle field – a number of the Lancastrian leaders, including Jasper's father, Owain, were executed after the battle, in the market square in Hereford.

Jasper refused to accept defeat, even after the complete annihilation of Lancastrian forces at the bloody Battle of Towton on Palm Sunday, 1461. Jasper himself was not present, instead, he was still in Wales, possibly at Harlech Castle (7). He emerged, together with the Duke of Exeter, in North Wales, where he lost a skirmish with Sir William Herbert at Twt Hill (9), on the outskirts of the coastal town of Caernarfon.

It is possible he hoped to attack Caernarfon itself – if he had managed to keep that under Lancastrian control, it would have made a convenient adjunct to Harlech, which was still holding out for Lancaster, and would have allowed troops to be landed on the north-west coast of Wales with ease. As it was, Herbert was victorious, and Jasper was obliged to slip away to join the Lancastrian court-in-exile in Scotland.

Over the following seven years, Jasper travelled constantly between Scotland, France, Brittany and Burgundy, liaising with the King of France, Queen Marguerite and King Henry. In 1462 he joined the besieged garrison of Bamburgh Castle (10) an enormous Norman keep on the north-east coast of England. The garrison was obliged to surrender on Christmas Eve 1462, with Jasper being granted a safe-conduct to return to Scotland. By 1464, the castle was again in Lancastrian hands, but was defeated in an early use of artillery by Richard Neville, Earl of Warwick. The castle was severely damaged, and what can be seen now is largely the restoration of the 18th and 19th centuries.

Bamburgh is in private hands, but is open to the public during March – October. Its location on the Northumbrian coast makes it worth a visit, just to admire the scenery.

By 1464, Henry VI was no longer welcome in Scotland, and his forces having been defeated first at Hedgeley Moor, and then at Hexham in April and May respectively, Henry was a fugitive. Jasper continued to travel between France and Wales. He carried out a swift raid on Denbigh Castle in 1468, burning the town to the ground, before retreating via Harlech.

This raid made Edward more determined than ever to capture Harlech, which eventually surrendered, after the longest siege ever conducted in mainland Britain. The famous Welsh song, 'Men of Harlech', commemorates it. Harlech Castle is one of the most spectacular of Edward I's castles in Wales. During the fifteenth century, the sea lapped its walls, but changes in the coastline mean it is now well over a mile from the shore. Its commanding position over Ceredigion Bay with a backdrop of Snowdonia make it a beautiful place to visit, despite its bloody and controversial history. It is in the care of Cadw (the

Welsh equivalent of English Heritage or Historic Scotland) and is open all year round.

In 1469, the Lancastrians entered England again, this time under the leadership of the Earl of Warwick, who had abandoned his Yorkist allegiance for entirely self-serving reasons, and Jasper, who was named as Joint Lieutenant of the Kingdom. Henry VI was briefly restored, but Edward IV won two crushing victories – first at Barnet, where Warwick was killed, and then at Tewkesbury where the young Edward of Lancaster, and the majority of the Lancastrian leaders were killed. Jasper, who had been recruiting in Wales, heard the news of the loss at Tewkesbury whilst at Chepstow Castle (11).

Chepstow is another of the castles built by the Norman Marcher Lords to secure their hold on the South Wales coast and the Severn and Wye valleys. Begun in 1067, it was extended continuously until around 1300. According to its managers, Cadw, it has the oldest wooden doors in Europe – dating from around 1200! It is open to the public.

In 1471, there was, of course, no Severn Bridge. Gloucester was the first crossing point, and it was here that the main Lancastrian force had planned to meet Jasper, before being forced to march on to Tewkesbury. They were travelling so quickly that there was no possibility that a message could reach Jasper in time to bring his men to Tewkesbury before the advancing Yorkists could catch up.

As soon as Edward realised that Jasper was not among the dead or captured, he sent Sir Roger Vaughan to capture him. Whether Edward remembered that Vaughan had been responsible for the execution of Owain Tudor is unknown – the King was renowned for his ability to remember names in every town he went to, so it is certainly possible that it was a deliberate provocation. But, if it was, it backfired on Vaughan as

Jasper, getting wind of his approach, took him before he himself could be arrested.

Vaughan was swiftly executed and Jasper, who had his nephew, Henry Tudor, with him, sped towards Pembroke Castle, whence after a brief siege, soon lifted by his allies, he made for Tenby.

The good relations he had fostered with the town ten years before now paid off as he and Henry were hidden in the cellars of a Mr White – probably the former mayor – before being spirited away to Brittany. It is alleged that the cellars underneath Boots the Chemist in Tenby is the very location where Jasper and Henry hid.

Jasper next set foot on Welsh soil on 7th August, 1485, when, together with his nephew and a small army, he landed at the port of Milford (12), now known as Milford Haven, on the north Pembrokeshire coast. From here, gathering men, they marched through west Wales, crossed into England at Shrewsbury and met Richard III on the battlefield at Bosworth (13) in Leicestershire. Bosworth, surprisingly, is not a well-documented battle, and there have been numerous theories as to exactly where the fighting took place. Today, there is an extensive interpretation centre, and research continues.

Once Henry Tudor was successfully established as King, Jasper received extensive rewards, including the dukedom of Bedford, his old earldom of Pembroke, and a rich wife, Katherine Woodville, Dowager Duchess of Buckingham. Whilst he was called upon to serve the King in government, and at the Battle of Stoke in 1487, and Henry's invasion of France in 1492, he settled himself largely at Sudeley Castle, Gloucestershire, and Thornbury Castle (14), also in Gloucestershire, one of Katherine's dower castles. Thornbury today is a country house hotel, the majority of which was constructed in the years after 1511 by Jasper's step-son, Edward, 3rd Duke of Buckingham.

Jasper chose to be buried in Somerset, in the Abbey of Keynsham (15), a house of Augustinian Canons, dedicated to the Virgin. The Abbey was dissolved in 1539, and, whilst traces of it remain, there is no sign of his tomb, which cost 100 marks.

The list below corresponds to the map which follows of places Jasper Tudor would have known.

Key to Map

1.   Bishop's Palace, Hatfield, Hertfordshire
2.   Barking Abbey, Greater London
3.   Pembroke Castle, Pembroke
4.   Palace of Westminster, London
5.   Tenby Town Walls, Tenby, Pembrokeshire
6.   Denbigh Castle, Denbigh, Clwyd
7.   Harlech Castle, Harlech, Gwynedd
8.   Mortimer's Cross, Wigmore, Herefordshire
9.   Twt Hill, Caernarfon, Gwynedd
10.   Bamburgh Castle, Northumberland
11.   Chepstow Castle, Gwent
12.   Milford Haven, Pembrokeshire
13.   Bosworth Field, Leicestershire
14.   Thornbury Castle, Gloucestershire
15.   Keynsham Abbey, Keynsham, Somerset

Map

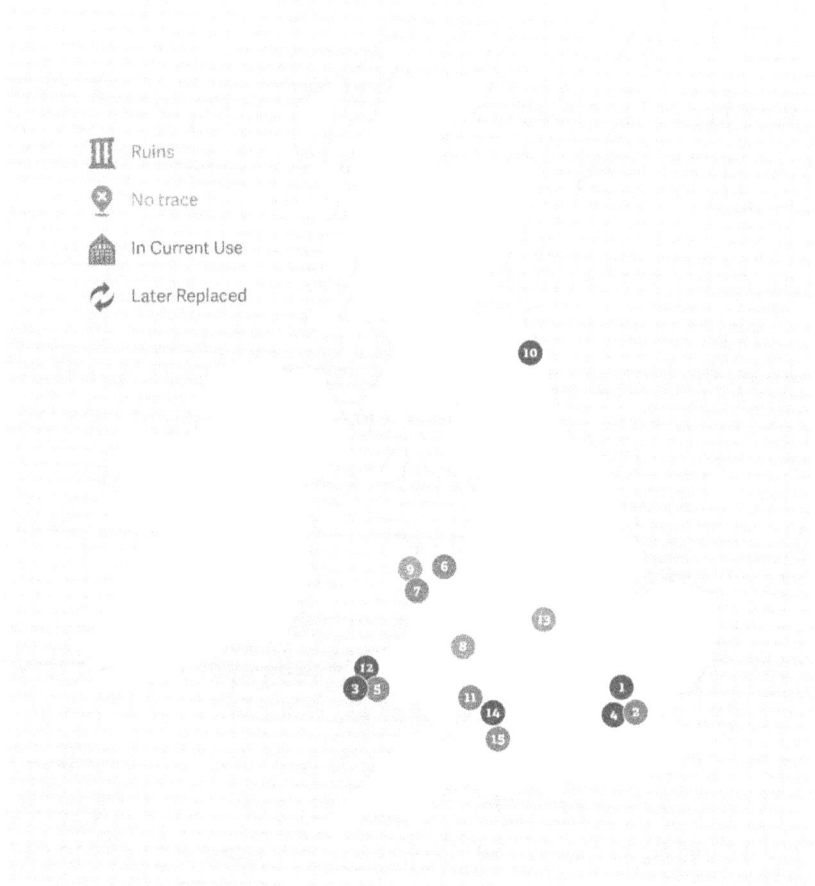

Chapter 22: Wales & the Wars of the Roses

We are going back further than the Tudor period in this chapter to look at how the political and social structure of Wales worked both for and against Jasper Tudor, Earl of Pembroke in his support, first for the House of Lancaster, then for his own Tudor nephew.

*

During the Middle Ages, Wales was not a single political state under one king as England became after the Norman conquest of 1066, but rather a fluctuating group of kingdoms, principalities and lordships.

The early Norman kings were not particularly interested in annexing Wales, but they wanted a route to Ireland along the south coast of Wales and a buffer zone along the border or 'march' with England. As the English crown did not have enough money or manpower to manage these areas, a type of landholding was developed called a Marcher Lordship. These were granted to senior Norman barons, who were then responsible for maintaining the border – in effect, any land they could win from the Welsh, belonged to them, but they owed allegiance to the King of England.

The area of Wales that did not fall under Norman control continued to be a group of principalities or lordships that sometimes converged under a strong leader, but, more often jostled amongst themselves for supremacy. There were various attempts under King John and Henry III to force the more powerful Welsh princes to accept English overlordship, but, until the time of Edward I (1239 – 1307) the relative strength of the Welsh and English within Wales fluctuated.

One of the aspects that weakened the ability of Wales to resist the English, was its system of inheritance of land. In England, the eldest son inherited everything, unless specific provisions were made for other children. Where there were no sons, female inheritance was recognised, initially with the oldest daughter taking all of the inheritance but later, with daughters being co-parcenors (splitting the inheritance). Illegitimate children had no rights of inheritance.

In Wales, the system was, in some ways, fairer – the land was divided between all of a man's sons, even if they were illegitimate. Less fairly, women could not inherit land at all. The upshot of this structure (known in English law as) was that it became difficult for a single individual to build up a coherent estate that he could pass on to one son.

The rules on inheritance applied to land, rather than titles. The crowns of the various kingdoms – Gwynedd, Deheubarth and Powys being the main ones - descended to the eldest son, if he were of age (late twenties) and without any physical or mental disabilities. Of course, inheriting the crown, but with only part of the lands his father had held, made succeeding generations weaker. If the eldest son were not considered a competent inheritor, any of his brothers, uncles or cousins to the second degree could either be chosen as leader or as frequently occurred, might snatch the crown.

Annexation by England

As may be imagined, the inheritance structure often created disputes, and English interference was often welcomed by one or other party to gain advantage over brothers or cousins. With hindsight, involving the English Crown can be seen as suicidal, but, presumably, it worked for men whose primary ambition was personal or familial, rather than national.

Thus when Llywelyn ap Gruffydd, who styled himself Prince of Aberffraw and Lord of Snowdon (effectively north and mid-Wales), achieved a measure of hegemony, his efforts at unification were undermined by Gwenwynwyn, Prince of Powys, who allied with the Edward I. This opened the door to the enemy, and by 1282, Edward, probably the most ruthless man ever to sit on the English throne, had annihilated Wales as an independent state, imposing, under the Statutes of Rhuddlan, English rule and English law in many areas (although not in inheritance, with the exception of excluding illegitimate sons. It no doubt suited Edward to keep the old system alive, to minimise the chances of a new strong leader arising).

Edward built a string of castles to surround Llywelyn's heartland of Gwynedd, including Denbigh, Rhuddlan, Conwy, Beaumaris, Caernarfon and Harlech, all enabling access by sea. Today, they are wonderful examples of the best mediaeval military architecture, but for some two hundred years, they were, for the Welsh, a symbol of oppression. Welshmen were not permitted to reside in the new towns that surrounded the castles.

In the late 1300s, the Welsh rose up under Owain Glyndwr (c. 1359 – c. 1415), a descendant of the Lord Rhys, Prince of Deheubarth. Glyndwr, from north-east Wales, was an established figure in the local gentry – mixing with the English marcher lords, as much as with his own Welsh kin. It is likely he was trained as a lawyer in England as well as fighting in the English army in Scotland.

Following a dispute with his arch-enemy, Lord Grey of Rhuthin, who arranged for Glyndwr to miss a summons for military service, making him, technically, a traitor to England, Glyndwr claimed his title as Prince of Powys and began a war that would last nine years and that had widespread support not just throughout Wales, but from Welshmen settled in England, who returned home in great numbers.

In 1402, in an attempt at retaliation, the Penal Laws against Wales were passed by the English Parliament. Welshmen could not hold senior crown offices, bear arms, or buy property in English towns (including those in Wales that had been established by Edward I). Education of Welsh children was restricted, and no public assemblies were permitted. These laws also applied to Englishmen who married Welsh women.

During the war, Glyndwr allied with Scotland, with France, and with the Mortimer earls of March (disgruntled because Richard II, who had named Edmund Mortimer as his heir, had been deposed by Henry IV of Lancaster). In 1404, Glyndwr called a Parliament at Machynlleth in mid-Wales, re-establishing Welsh law, and being crowned as Prince of Wales.

But Wales had insufficient men, money or armaments to effectively expel the English over the long term. By 1405, Glyndwr's French allies had retreated, and in 1409, Edmund Mortimer, married to Glyndwr's daughter, Catrin, was killed in the last battle of the war, at Harlech Castle. Owain's wife and two of his daughters were imprisoned in the Tower of London, and never released.

Despite this set-back, Owain fought on, but disappeared from view in 1415. Never captured, his memory was kept alive by the bards who travelled between the courts of the Welsh gentry, reciting his glories, but also encouraging the Welsh to be ready to support a new Welsh leader. The British kings of myth and legend– Cadwallader and Arthur – were now joined by a new hero, Glyndwr, and the bards sang that one of them would come again in the hour of greatest need and drive the Saxons out of Britain. The Welsh were therefore being primed to look for the 'mab darogan', the son of prophesy, and it was into this dream that the Tudors would tap to take Henry Tudor to the throne.

Welsh Lancastrians & Yorkists

Not all Welshmen supported Glyndwr, a notable exception being Dafydd ap Llywelyn (sometimes referred to as Dafydd Gam), one of Henry IV's strongest supporters in Wales. Captured by Glyndwr, he was ransomed, and went on to fight at Agincourt. His daughter, Gwladys ferch Dafydd married first, Sir Roger Vaughan, and then William ap Thomas of Raglan. Gwladys' sons played an important role in the Wars of the Roses, and, from having been members of Jasper Tudor's council, became his sworn enemies.

The advent of Henry V brought a slight improvement in Anglo-Welsh relations – Henry was far more interested in conquering France than he was in the rocky uplands of Wales, and, although the Penal Laws were not abolished, they were imposed less harshly.

It is against this back-drop of the Welsh wars that the secret marriage of Katherine de Valois, widow of Henry V, needs to be seen. Owain Tudor, who may have been in Henry V's army or household at one time, was the son of Owain Glyndwr's cousin. It was no wonder that the King's relatives, particularly his brother, Humphrey of Gloucester were horrified. Not just Owain's relative poverty and nationality, but that he was closely related to the arch-rebel himself, made a bitter pill.

Owain's sons, Edmund and Jasper, were brought up as English aristocrats, rather than the descendants of Welsh princes. After Katherine's death, Owain had been imprisoned and then harried back to Wales, so Jasper's childhood memories of his father were probably dim. Nevertheless, Owain came to feel as grateful to his step-son, Henry VI, as Edmund and Jasper did. Once he was old enough, the King pardoned Owain for his offence in marrying Katherine, and treated him honourably. The King also granted Edmund and Jasper the valuable earldoms of Richmond and Pembroke respectively, as well as the wardship of his wealthy cousin, Lady Margaret Beaufort.

No details are known of Owain and Jasper Tudor's personal relationship, other than that they fought together at Mortimer's Cross, and that Jasper revenged himself on the man who ordered Owain's execution. In his will, Jasper gave money to the church in which Owain was buried – the Greyfriars at Hereford.

So at the outbreak of hostilities, there were Lancastrian supporters, such as Jasper Tudor and Dafydd Gam, and others who were mindful of the Mortimer claim to the throne, now embodied in Richard, Duke of York. But cutting across any loyalty to English royal houses, were the conflicts and quarrels of a small society, widely inter-married, with competing loyalties, where blood feuds could continue for generations.

A case in point is the Herbert family, who became Jasper's greatest rivals for influence in South Wales. Sir William Herbert (known in Welsh as Gwilym Ddu – Black Will) was the son of Thomas ap Gwilym, who created the mighty edifice of Raglan Castle. Thomas ap Gwilym's second wife, and the mother of William, was Gwladys, daughter of Dafydd Gam with whom he had fought at Agincourt, together with Gwladys' first husband, Roger Vaughan.

Gwladys was a great patron of the traditional Welsh bardic culture, and was much feted in poetry, called *'the star of Abergavenny'* probably as much for her generosity to the bards as for her beauty. William Herbert inherited this taste, and his court at Raglan castle was very much a traditional Welsh court.

Given their parents' Lancastrian associations, it might have been expected, therefore, that William Herbert and his Vaughan half-brothers (Walter, Thomas and Roger) would be Lancastrians, but all of them became adherents of York, with William Herbert also marrying Anne

Devereux, daughter of Sir Walter Devereux, Lord Chancellor of Ireland, who held lands from York, and served under him.

William Herbert and another Thomas Vaughan (not his half-brother, but probably a relative) were members of Jasper's Council as Earl of Pembroke in the mid-1450s but the relationship broke down at some point.

It may be that the Herberts and Vaughans resented the incursion of Edmund and Jasper Tudor, brought up as English aristocrats, whose Welsh family were from the north, and who had no local affinity. Whilst this is mere speculation, it is not difficult to imagine that the Tudor brothers, in their early twenties, half-brothers to the King and probably brought up to think of any Welshman other than their father as being practically a savage, might have thrown their weight about in a way that aggravated experienced men and drove them into the arms of York.

Additionally, with York having a wide range of estates, not just those in Wales, he was more likely to hand over power and responsibility to Herbert and his family, whilst the Tudors seemed inclined to remain on the spot.

Regardless of how they arrived at their decision, Herbert and the Vaughans supported York faithfully, carrying that allegiance over to Edward IV. Black Will Herbert grew hugely in influence during the reign of Edward IV. Despite the twenty year age gap, the men became friends, and Herbert was granted extensive power and position, including the wardship of Jasper's nephew, Henry Tudor, after the Battle of Mortimer's Cross in 1461, which must have been a bitter blow for Jasper, and Jasper's earldom of Pembroke in 1468 after Herbert finally captured Harlech Castle in 1468

The young Henry Tudor lived from the age of four until he was twelve, at Herbert's seat at Raglan, together with Herbert's children, another

William, Maud (whom it was thought that Henry would marry) and Katherine. Henry Tudor was not Herbert's only Lancastrian ward – there was also Henry Percy, Earl of Northumberland, a very valuable prize. As a further mark of favour from Edward IV, William Herbert the Younger, was married to Edward IV's own sister-in-law, Mary Woodville, in 1466.

Ebb & Flow of Loyalties

The growing power of Herbert in South Wales was perceived as a threat by the Earl of Warwick, who also had extensive holdings in the area. Warwick destroyed this rival by having Herbert and his brother, Richard, executed after the Battle of Edgecote, on 26th July 1469, when Warwick's men defeated Edward IV's supporters. Mary Woodville's father and brother were also executed..

Following Edward IV's restoration to the throne in 1471, the new earl, Black Will's son, remained closely allied to the Yorkist cause, even after being requested to relinquish the earldom of Pembroke and accept the less valuable earldom of Huntingdon instead.

Black Will's half-brothers, the Vaughans, remained faithful to Edward IV, and then to his son, Edward V. Their kinsman, the Thomas Vaughan who had been Jasper's councillor, was appointed as Chamberlain to the young Prince Edward as soon as Edward IV was restored to the crown in 1471, and remained with the prince at Ludlow. Thomas Vaughan was arrested as he accompanied the young Edward to London, after the death of the King, by Richard, Duke of Gloucester, and executed in June 1483 although well into his seventies. This may have been one of the motivating factors for Herbert's failure to support Richard III.

The other family which influenced events in South Wales during the Wars of the Roses, was that of Gruffydd ap Nicolas. From an obscure background, Gruffydd was part of the affinity of Humphrey, Duke of

Gloucester, until Gloucester's downfall and subsequent death in 1447 when Gruffydd was imprisoned. Like many of Gloucester's erstwhile colleagues, he was then associated with the Duke of York. Gruffydd's contribution to Welsh life – the patronising of *eisteddfodau* (assemblies for hearing and judging poetry) and support of individual bards affected politics. Bards, in a sense, were PR agents – they wrote positive verses about their patrons and denigrated their enemies. They kept memories alive and stirred up the population. In particular the famous bard, Lewis Glyn Cothi, was a friend of Gruffydd's son, Owain, and wrote numerous verses in support of Jasper Tudor.

Thus, when Sir William Herbert, Earl of Pembroke, was killed after the Battle of Edgecote, by Warwick, the bards called on Jasper to avenge his death. It did not matter that Jasper and William supported opposing sides in the War – so far as the bards were concerned, their hero had been killed, and it was every good Welshman's job to take vengeance. The bards began to look again for the man who would deliver them from English domination.

Gruffydd had several sons, of whom Owain and Thomas were the most notorious – the word is used advisedly as father and sons were frequently the subject of complaints about their abuse of power. York had no control over Gruffydd, who garrisoned Carreg Cennen, Carmarthen and Aberystwyth castles, refusing to hand it over to York, who had the office of constable of the castle. Gruffydd then proceeded to indulge in a private war with Edmund Tudor, now Earl of Richmond. When Richmond eventually took Carmarthen from Gruffydd, he was, in turn besieged by Herbert and his brother-in-law, Devereux.

Gruffydd and his sons were granted a pardon in 1456 by Queen Marguerite of Anjou, and following this, the family largely became Lancastrian supporters, complicated by the fact that Thomas ap

Gruffydd's daughter, Margaret, married Sir William Herbert's brother, Richard. Owain and Thomas ap Gruffydd, working with Jasper Tudor, refused to surrender the Carreg Cennen Castle to the victorious Edward IV after Towton, but were eventually forced out, in 1462, after which, together with Thomas' son Rhys, they spent some time in exile in Burgundy.

Restored to their lands by the Readeption of Henry VI, they retained them after the defeat of the Lancastrians, and came to an accommodation with Edward IV. By 1474, Rhys ap Thomas had inherited his father's lands (his older brothers having died).

The Triumph of the Red Dragon

In 1483, Buckingham's revolt against Richard III was not supported by Rhys or any other Welshmen, so far as can be ascertained. There was no possibility that Buckingham, an unpopular man, and an Englishman to boot, could be the '*Mab darogan*' who would rescue the Welsh from their ancient Saxon enemies (it is fair to say that the bards were not a race who believed in forgiving and forgetting past wrongs!).

Richard III rewarded Rhys with new offices and an annuity of 40 marks. He also requested that Rhys' son be sent to Richard – the word hostage was not used, but the meaning was clear. Rhys declined, informing Richard that nothing could bind him more strongly than his conscience. Either Rhys' conscience was rather elastic, or he had already sworn to support Henry Tudor.

For the Herberts, the advent of Richard III had led to the disinheritance, and probably death of Lady Herbert's nephew, Edward V, the shaming of her sister, Queen Elizabeth, who was accused of living in adultery, and the execution of their connection, Sir Thomas Vaughan, Edward V's chamberlain, in his seventies. Sir William Herbert, son of Black Will, now Earl of Huntingdon, had been Henry's companion as a boy, and it appears that Henry agreed that, if he could not marry one of the daughters of Edward IV, he would marry Katherine Herbert, Maud already being married to the Earl of Northumberland. On the other hand, Herbert had received Richard III's illegitimate daughter, Katherine, as a bride, together with the position of Justiciar of South Wales, so making a decision between the two parties was not easy.

In 1485, all of these strands of conflicting loyalties, family connections, memories of past wrongs, and the desire to regain Welsh autonomy came together to give Henry Tudor a springboard from which he could conquer and take the crown. During the preceding year, messengers had scurried between Wales, Brittany, and later France, as Henry began his campaign.

On his arrival, Henry hoped to be joined by both Rhys and Huntingdon, but, initially, there was no sign of them and Henry and Jasper kept to the west coast of Wales, rather than crossing into the territories controlled by them. It soon became clear, however, that the Rhys, together with Huntingdon's brother, was marching in parallel with Henry.

Unable to discern their ultimate intentions, Henry sent men to negotiate, and eventually, on 16th August, 1485, not just Rhys ap Thomas, but a flock of the North Welsh gentry joined Henry. It's not clear exactly what happened to Walter Herbert, but it appears that none of the Herbert family fought at Bosworth, for either side.

After the battle of Bosworth, it was claimed, by the bard, Guto'r Glyn, that Rhys himself had killed Richard III, 'he killed the boar (Richard's badge was the White Boar of Gloucester), shaved his head.' The recent forensic investigation of Richard's remains certainly suggest that among his wounds was a slicing cut along his scalp.

The support of Rhys ap Thomas was a defining factor in Henry's success and Henry himself made frequent references to his Welsh ancestry, carrying the Red Dragon banner of Cadwallader into battle and showing his arms as supported by the red dragon. He also appointed many Welshmen to his household and to public office, some ninety years after the Penal laws had prohibited the Welsh from holding senior office.

Nevertheless, the advent of the Tudors did not prove to be the panacea that the Welsh bards had hoped for, and, in the Acts of Union of 1536 – 1542, Wales was divided up into shires on the English model with the abolition of the Marcher Lordships. The upside was that the shires could now elect members to Parliament, but, all public business, including in the law courts, had to be conducted in English, according to English law. The custom of inheritance by all sons was abolished, and the English rule of primogeniture introduced.

Chapter 23: Two Book Reviews

Jasper has recently been the focus of sustained attention by biographers. We have reviewed two of them here.

Jasper Tudor: Godfather of the Tudor Dynasty

Author: Debra Bayani

Publisher: Made Global Publishing Ltd

In a nutshell A readable account of Jasper Tudor's life with interesting source material – a bit repetitious in parts.

Jasper Tudor has recently been the subject of three biographies. This one, the first non-fiction work published by Ms Bayani, has a readable style and the book is well illustrated with some lovely original photographs, taken by the author, which show many of the places that figure in Jasper's life.

Jasper's life was so eventful, that is it difficult not to think that some of his exploits are made up – the escapes from besieged castles, the daring raids into Yorkist held Wales in the 1460s and the good fortune that saved him from being handed over to Edward IV, but, in fact, all of the events described are well-attested. Despite the drama of Jasper's life, Ms Bayani never falls into the temptation of speculating about his feelings or emotions.

The book opens with the political background in France in the youth of Jasper's mother, Katherine de Valois, who was married to Henry V as part of the Treaty of Troyes, to end the war in France. It then covers Katherine's widowhood and marriage to Owain Tudor. Ms Bayani effectively brings evidence to show that it was believed at the time that a marriage between Katherine and Owain had taken place, despite later commentators suggesting that their children were illegitimate. She also convincingly contradicts speculation that Jasper's brother, Edmund, was in fact the son of Edmund Beaufort.

Ms Bayani has then obviously undertaken a good deal of research – bringing together many details of Jasper's estates and income, and tracing his movements, so far as possible, to give a picture of the part he played in the Wars of the Roses, and in the years of guerrilla warfare of the 1460s.

Where Ms Bayani's lack of experience as a historian occasionally shows is in her failure to analyse some of her sources. She states confidently on one page that Jasper had a mistress and illegitimate children, naming them and giving an account of their lives, then a couple of pages later, says that there was no contemporary evidence of their existence, nor any provision for any children in Jasper's will. She doesn't conclude the discussion by giving arguments for or against their existence.

The writing style is easy and pleasant, although occasionally it is a bit repetitious – the same event is covered two or three times, in slightly different words. Again, this is probably a fault of inexperience, which I am sure will improve with time. I can honestly say that I am looking forward to reading Ms Bayani's next work.

Jasper Tudor: Dynasty Maker

Author: Terry Breverton

Publisher: Amberley Publishing

In a nutshell: A fantastically detailed look at the Wars of the Roses in the context of a man who never wavered in his allegiance, and whose tenacity ensured the ultimate triumph of Henry Tudor.

Terry Breverton is the author of a wide range of books with topics as diverse as pirates, herbals and the First World War. His specialism, however, is Welsh topics, and his comprehensive research into the Welsh experience of the Wars of the Roses, and the reaction of Wales to calls from both Lancastrian and Yorkist kings, gives a whole new perspective to the conflict. Breverton concentrates on the life of Jasper Tudor, second son of Queen Catherine de Valois by her second husband, Owain Tudor. Jasper was one of the few men present at both the opening battle of the War – St Albans in 1455 and the final confrontation at Stoke in 1487.

Jasper, like his older brother, Edmund, received recognition and a generous endowment from his half-brother, Henry VI. Breverton looks at Jasper's early career and discovers that, during the 1440s and 1450s, far from being a blind partisan of Henry's inept government, he was on good terms with Richard of York, and sought to support York's attempts to improve it. It was not until the Yorkists took up arms against the King that Jasper firmly committed himself to fight for his half-brother.

Breverton has undertaken extensive research into the government offices and landholdings in Wales, and how they changed hands over the course of the wars – he identifies three great power bases – Jasper's own, which he continued to control to a degree until the defeat of the Lancasatrians at Tewkesbury in 1571; that of William Herbert (or Gwilym Du, '*Black William*', in his native Welsh) and that of Rhys ap Thomas. Herbert was originally part of Jasper's own affinity, but shifted his allegiance to Edward IV, and was rewarded with Jasper's earldom of Pembroke. He also became the guardian of Jasper's nephew, Henry Tudor. Even more than in England, the personally loyalty of men to their lord affected their willingness to fight for the lord's chosen side. Nowhere is this more clearly shown than in the reaction of Wales to the revolt of the Duke of Buckingham against Richard III in 1483.

Buckingham, although he had been granted wide-ranging powers in the country had little or no personal following among the Welsh, who largely ignored the uprising. It was a different story when Jasper and Henry Tudor arrived in 1485 – the Herberts, who were Yorkists made no attempt to prevent his march, Rhys ap Thomas, who had been a Yorkist actively supported him, and the northern counties of Denbighshire and Flintshire, under the leadership of the Stanleys also fell in behind the Red Dragon banner.

Breverton makes use of a wide range of Welsh bardic and literary sources – which, although less well known, are not necessarily more, or less, accurate that the English sources despite often being written in poetic style, rather than as factual accounts. The language used in them illustrates pent up anger in Wales against the conquest of the country and the vicious penal laws enacted against Owain Glyndwr at the turn of the fifteenth century. The prophesies of a Welshman who would free them from the Saxon yoke was a dream that many could follow. Had Henry and Jasper landed in England they would have been far less likely to gather the number of troops they did before crossing the border.

Following the victory at Bosworth for which Henry VII could thank Jasper, and that other Lancastrian stalwart, the Earl of Oxford, Jasper was the only man granted a dukedom and was showered with land (including Sudeley Castle) and offices from his grateful nephew. He was also granted a wife, connected to the family of Edward IV. Katherine Woodville, widow of the Duke of Buckingham, was in her late twenties, compared with Jasper's fifty-four, but the fact that she was aunt to Elizabeth of York, whom Henry had vowed to marry, strengthened the relationship between the formerly warring factions. At no time does Breverton speculate on Jasper's private life (fifty-four being extremely old for a noble to marry for the first time in the fifteenth century). He mentions the theory that Jasper had been in love with his sister-in-law, Margaret Beaufort, but suggests that the most likely reason is that the Wars of the Roses had begun before a suitable bride had been found, and that Jasper had not had time subsequently to marry. Marriage to Katherine was also a way of providing Jasper with a very fine income as the Duchess' dower rights (confiscated by Richard III) were returned.

Breverton's interpretations of Jasper's character are limited to observations where he believes he has direct evidence – he contends that Jasper was of a conciliatory nature and encouraged Henry VII to seek reconciliation with the Yorkists rather than another round of blood-letting, citing the easy terms given by Jasper to the adherents of Francis Lovell's rather lack-lustre rebellion in early 1486.

Jasper's final years as Henry's most trusted advisor (except for Margaret Beaufort) are covered – including his final military command – an expedition into France that ended with a peace treaty. He also acted as deputy for the infant Arthur, Prince of Wales in the Council of Wales, based at Ludlow.

I really enjoyed this book – the wealth of detail, the Welsh perspective – so little considered elsewhere – and, in good Welsh fashion, the minutiae of familial relationships between the various men of Jasper's affinity. I have only one negative comment – the book is long, and there is very frequent repetition of the same fact, even the same sentence over several pages. A good edit would remove these annoyances, and make the narrative flow more tightly.

Bibliography

Bayani, Debra, *Jasper Tudor: Godfather of the Tudor Dynasty*, Kindle (Made Global Publishing, 2015)

Breverton, Terry, *Jasper Tudor: Dynasty Maker*, 1st edn (Gloucestershire: Amberley Publishing, 2015)

De Lisle, Leanda, *Tudor: The Family Story* (United Kingdom: Chatto & Windus, 2013)

Gristwood, Sarah, *Blood Sisters: The Hidden Lives of the Women Behind the Wars of the Roses,* Kindle (HarperPress, 2013)

Jones, Dan, *The Hollow Crown: The Wars of the Roses and the Rise of The Tudors*, 1st edn (United Kingdom: Faber & Faber Non-Fiction, 2014)

Jones, Michael K, and Malcolm G Underwood, *The King's Mother: Lady Margaret Beaufort, Countess of Richmond and Derby*, 1st edn (New York: Cambridge University Press, Cambridge, 1991)

Roberts, Sara Elin, *Jasper: The Tudor Kingmaker*, Kindle (Fonthill Media, 2015)

Skidmore, Chris, *Bosworth: The Birth of the Tudors*, 1st edn (London: W&N, 2014)

www.ingramcontent.com/pod-product-compliance
Lightning Source LLC
Chambersburg PA
CBHW020514030426
42337CB00011B/382